Hacking University Computer Hacking and Learning Python 2 Manuscript Bundle

Essential Beginners Guide on How to Become an Amateur Hacker and Learn Python Programming From Scratch

Series: Hacking Freedom and Data Driven (Freshman & Junior)

By Isaac D. Cody

QUICK TABLE OF CONTENTS

This book will contain 2 manuscripts from the Hacking Freedom and Data Driven series. It will essentially be two books into one.

The Freshman Edition will cover the basics of hacking in general such as hacking wifi, malware, and several types of hacking attacks.

Hacking University Junior Edition welcomes you to the programming art of Python.

Both books are for intended for beginner's and even those with moderate experience with Hacking and Python programming.

Hacking University: Freshman Edition

Essential Beginner's Guide on How to Become an Amateur Hacker (Hacking, How to Hack, Hacking for Beginners, Computer Hacking)

Series: Hacking Freedom and Data Driven Volume 1

By Isaac D. Cody

© **Copyright 2014 by Isaac D. Cody- All rights reserved.**

This document is geared towards providing exact and reliable information in regards to the topic and issue covered. The publication is sold with the idea that the publisher is not required to render accounting, officially permitted, or otherwise, qualified services. If advice is necessary, legal or professional, a practiced individual in the profession should be ordered.

- From a Declaration of Principles which was accepted and approved equally by a Committee of the American Bar Association and a Committee of Publishers and Associations.

In no way is it legal to reproduce, duplicate, or transmit any part of this document in either electronic means or in printed format. Recording of this publication is strictly prohibited and any storage of this document is not allowed unless with written permission from the publisher. All rights reserved.

The information provided herein is stated to be truthful and consistent, in that any liability, in terms of inattention or otherwise, by any usage or abuse of any policies, processes, or directions contained within is the solitary and utter responsibility of the recipient reader. Under no circumstances will any legal responsibility or blame be held against the publisher for any reparation, damages, or monetary loss due to the information herein, either directly or indirectly.

Respective authors own all copyrights not held by the publisher.

The information herein is offered for informational purposes solely, and is universal as so. The presentation of the information is without contract or any type of guarantee assurance.

The trademarks that are used are without any consent, and the publication of the trademark is without permission or backing by the trademark owner. All trademarks and brands within this book are for clarifying purposes only and are the owned by the owners themselves, not affiliated with this document.

Table of Contents

Preview

Introduction

Chapter 1: History and Famous Hacks

Chapter 2: Modern Security

Chapter 3: Common Terms

Chapter 4: Getting Started Hacking

Chapter 5: Building Skill and Protecting Oneself

Conclusion

Preview

Do you ever wonder what the future holds in terms of computer security and computer hacking? Have you ever wondered if hacking is right for you?

It is estimated that a Certified Ethical Hacker earns on average $71,000. Differentiate yourself and learn what it means to become a hacker!

This book will provide you the ultimate guide in how to actually start and begin how to learn Computer Hacking. I firmly believe with the right motivation, ethics, and passion, *anyone* can be a hacker.

"Hacking University: Freshman Edition. Essential Beginner's Guide on How to Become an Amateur Hacker will encompass a wide array of topics that will lay

<u>the foundation of computer hacking AND *actually* enable you to start hacking.</u>

Some of the topics covered in this book include:

- **The History of Hacking**

- **Benefits and Dangers of Hacking**

- **The Future of Cybersecurity**

- **Essential Basics to Start Hacking**

- **Computer Networks**

- **Hacking in terms of Hardware and Software**

- **Penetration Testing**

- **Cracking Passwords**

- **Backdoors**

- **Trojans**

- **Information Security**

- **Network Scan and VPN**

- **Viruses**

Believe it or not there are just a few of the topics covered in this book. "Hacking University: Freshman Edition. Essential Beginner's Guide on How to Become an Amateur Hacker (Hacking, How to Hack, Hacking for Beginners, Computer Hacking) will cover much more related topics to this.

Introduction

I want to thank you and congratulate you for downloading the book Hacking University: Freshman Edition. This book is the definitive starters guide for information on hacking. Whether you are a security professional or an aspiring hacktivist, this book provides you with definitions, resources, and demonstrations for the novice.

Hacking is a divisive subject, but it is a matter of fact that hacking is used for benevolent purposes as well as malevolent. Hacking is needed, for otherwise how would incompetence and abuse be brought to light? Equally, the "Hacker's Manifesto" explains the ideology of hackers- they are guilty of no crime, save curiosity. Experimenting with systems is inherently fun, and it offers exceptionally gifted people an outlet for their inquisitiveness. This book continues those ethics; the demonstrations made available here are written in good faith for the sake of education and enjoyment.

Nonetheless federal governments hack each other to steal classified information, groups hack corporations on a political agenda, and individuals exploit other people for revenge. These examples do not represent hackers, and the aforementioned scenarios are not what good-natured, curious hackers would do. This book does not condone these types of hacks either.

As a disclaimer, though- nobody is responsible for any damage caused except for yourself. Some demonstrations in this book are potentially dangerous, so by performing them you are doing so willingly of your own accord and with explicit permission from the computer and network owners.

And for the non-hackers reading, there's an inescapable fact- you will need the information in this book to protect yourself. You will learn what hackers look for and how they exploit security weaknesses. Therefore, you will be able to protect yourself more fully from their threats. Lastly, if you do not develop your knowledge in this field, you will inevitably fall behind. Complacency leads to vulnerability in the computer world, so this book could be the one that clues you in on just how important security and hacking are.

It's time for you to become an amazing hacker. Studying the history of the art form will give you an appreciation and background, so we will begin there. Read on and begin your career of security.

Chapter 1: History and Famous Hacks

Hacking has a rich a varied history beginning far back in ancient times. Cryptography and encryption (passwords) were used by Roman armies. A commander would need to send orders across the battlefield and would do so by writing instructions on a piece of paper. Foot-soldiers could run the papers back and forth and thus one side would gain an advantage with increased knowledge.

Undoubtedly the soldiers would sometimes be captured and the secret orders would fall into the wrong hands. To combat this, commanders began obscuring the text by transforming and moving around the letters. This process, known as encryption, succeeded in confusing enemy commanders until they were forced to attempt to break the encryption. Employing mathematical methods and clever tricks to un-obfuscate the orders, the enemy would sometimes be able to decode the text. Therefore, ancient people were hacking long before computers were even conceived!

However, when most people imagine early hacking, they are usually drawn to the wildly interesting story of the Enigma Machine. The Enigma machine was a device used famously in Nazi Germany during the 2nd World War to encrypt and decrypt war messages. Much like the ancient Romans, the German messages were obfuscated and transformed before sending so that if the message might be intercepted, the opposition would be unable to read the highly secretive text. Besides a brief moment in the 1930's where the encryption method was discovered, the Enigma machine was very successful for much of its existence. Polish cryptologists were the ones to initially break the code, but Germany countered later in the decade by improving on the design and making Enigma far more complicated.

The rein of Enigma continued throughout the war. An American professor by the name of Alan Turing used his studies and extensive knowledge of mathematics to provide key research that broke the Enigma code again in 1939. As it usually is with encryption methods though, Enigma was improved again and made unbreakable until 1943 when Turing assisted the Navy and produced a faster decryption machine.

"Bombes", as they were called, were the decryption machines the facilitated cracking the Enigma code. Bombe machines used rotating drums and electrical signals to analyze the scrambled messages and output the correct configuration of dials and plugs that would result in a decoded text. Bombes could almost be considered some of the earliest computers due to their mechanical and electrical complexity. Despite the highly advanced technology put forth from both sides, Enigma's final demise actually came about from the allied capture of the secret keys, or codes, used in the machine. With the encryption method clear, Enigma became mostly useless baring another redesign. A redesign couldn't come soon enough, as the war soon ended. The allied ability to decode Enigma messages definitely played a large part in their success.

After World War II, an immense amount of research and calculations went into developing projectile missiles and nuclear weapons. The Cold War essentially facilitated the development of modern electrical computers because electronic devices could perform mathematics at a speedy pace. Advanced devices such as Colossus, ENIAC, and EDSAC paved the way for faster electronics throughout the 1950s and 1960s. Supercomputers were used in universities and corporations around the world, and these early devices were susceptible to intrusion and hacking as well. However, the most notable 20th century hacking movement was known as Phreaking, and it involved "hacking" through telephones.

Phreaking began after phone companies switched from human operators to automated switches. Automated switches determined where to route a phone call based on the tonal frequency generated by telephones when numbers were dialed. The pitched beeps heard when pressing buttons on cell phones is reminiscent of this, as each button produces a differently pitched tone. Tones in succession dialed numbers with automatic switches, and the phone user would have their call connected to the number dialed.

Certain other tones translated to different actions, though- phreakers discovered that by imitating the special tones they could control the automated switches and get free long-distance phone calls across the world. Phreaking then evolved into a culture of individuals who would explore and experiment with phone systems, often delving into illegal methods to have fun and evade fees. Skilled phreakers could even eavesdrop on phone calls and manipulate phone company employees by impersonating technical staff.

A few phreakers became famous within the community for discovering new techniques and furthering the phreaking study. Joseph Engressia was the first to discover the tone needed to make long distance calls, and John "Captain Crunch" Draper found that a prize whistle within a cereal box produced that exact tone, and he gained his nickname from that finding. Interviews of prominent phreakers inspired later generations- Steve Jobs himself liked to partake in the hobby.

Networked computers and the invention of BBS brought the culture to even more people, so the pastime grew tremendously. No longer a small movement, the government took notice in 1990 when phreaking communities were targeted by the United States Secret Service through Operation Sundevil. The operation saw a few phreaking groups shut down for illegal activity. As time progressed, landlines became increasingly less popular having to compete with cell phones, so phreaking mostly died in the 1990s. Mostly, phreaking culture sidestepped and got absorbed into hacking culture when personal computers became affordable to most families.

By the mid-1980s, corporations and government facilities were being hacked into regularly by hobbyists and "white-hat" professionals who report computer vulnerabilities. Loyd Blankenship wrote the "Hacker Manifesto" on an online magazine viewed by hackers and phreakers in 1986; the document later became a key piece in the philosophy of hackers as it attributes them as curious individuals who are not guilty of crime. Hacking continued to develop and in 1988 Robert Morris created a computer worm that crashed Cornell University's computer system. Although likely not malicious, this situation marked a division in computer hacking. Some individuals continued to have fun as "white-hats" and others sought illegal personal gain as "black-hat" hackers.

The most popular hacker group today is most definitely Anonymous. The aptly-named group is essentially hidden and member-less because it performs "operations" that any person can join, usually by voluntarily joining a botnet and DDoSing (these terms will be discussed further in subsequent chapters). Anonymous is most popular for their "raids" on Habbo Hotel, scientology, and Paypal. While some actions the group take seem contradictory to past action or counter-intuitive, these facts make sense because Anonymous does not have a defined membership and actions are taken by individuals claiming to be part of the group- there are no core members. Many news outlets label Anonymous as a terrorist group, and constant hacking operations keep the group in the public eye today.

Edward Snowden became a household name in 2013 when he leaked sensitive documents from the National Security Agency that revealed the US government's domestic and worldwide surveillance programs. Snowden is hailed as a hero by those that believe the surveillance was unwarranted, obtrusive, and an invasion of privacy. Opponents of Snowden claim he is a terrorist who leaked private data of the government. No matter which way the situation is viewed, it becomes clear that hacking and cybersecurity are grand-scale issues in the modern world.

Having always-connected internet has exposed almost every computer as vulnerable. Cybersecurity is now a major concern for every government, corporation, and individual. Hacking is a necessary entity in the modern world, no matter if it is used for "good" or "evil". As computers are so prevalent and interweaved with typical function, hackers will be needed constantly for professional security positions. It is only through studying the past, though, that we can learn about the unique situation that modern hacking is in.

Chapter 2: Modern Security

IT professionals today usually do not fill "jack-of-all-trades" positions in corporations. While a small business may still employ a single person who is moderately proficient in most areas of technology, the huge demands imposed on internet connected big businesses means that several IT specialists must be present concurrently. Low-level help-desk personnel report to IT managers who report to administrators who report to the CTO (Chief Technology Officer). Additionally, sometimes there are even further specializations where security employees confer with administrators and report to a CIO (Chief Information Officer) or CSO (Chief Security Officer). Overall, security must be present in companies either full-time, contracted through a 3rd party, or through dual specialization of a system administrator. Annually a large amount of revenue is lost due to data breaches, cyber-theft, DDOS attacks, and ransomware. Hackers perpetuate the constant need for security while anti-hackers play catch-up to protect assets.

The role of a security professional is to confirm to the best of their ability the integrity of all the security of an organization. Below are a few explanations of the various areas of study that security professionals protect from threats. Some of these "domains" are also the key areas of study for CISSP (Certified Information System Security Professional) certificate holders, which is a proof of proficiency in security. CISSPs are sometimes considered anti-hackers because they employ their knowledge to stop hackers before the problem can even occur.

Network Security

Network security includes protecting a networked server from outside intrusion. This means that there cannot be any entry point for curious individuals to gain access. Data sent through the network should not be able to be intercepted or read, and sometimes encryption is needed to ensure compromised data is not useful to a hacker.

Access Control

A sophisticated security infrastructure needs to be able to identify and authenticate authorized individuals. Security professionals use methods such as passwords, biometrics, and two-factor authentication to make sure that a computer user really is who they say they are. Hackers attempt to disguise themselves as another user by stealing their password or finding loopholes.

Software Application Security

Hackers are quick to exploit hidden bugs and loopholes in software that could elevate their privilege and give them access to secret data. Since most corporations and governments run their own in-house proprietary software, security professionals cannot always fully test software for problems. This is a popular areas for hackers to exploit, because bugs and loopholes are potentially numerous.

Disaster Recovery

Sometimes the hacker is successful. A skilled troublemaker can infiltrate remote servers and deal great damage or steal a plethora of information; disaster recovery is how security professionals respond. Often, there are documents that have a specific plan for most common disaster situations. Automated recognition systems can tell when an intrusion has occurred or when data has been stolen, and the best CISSPs can shut down the hack or even reverse-track the culprit to reveal their true identity. Disaster recovery is not always a response to attacks, though. Natural disasters count too, and there is nothing worse than a flooded server room. Professionals must have a disaster plan to get their business back up and running or else the business could face a substantial loss of money.

Encryption and Cryptography

As we've learned by looking at history, the encryption of data is a valuable tool that can protect the most valuable information. For every encryption method, though, there is a hacker/cracker using their talents to break it. Security personnel use cryptography to encrypt sensitive files, and hackers break that encryption. Competent hackers can break weak encryption by having a strong computer (that can perform fast math), or by finding flaws in the encryption algorithms.

Risk Management

Is it worth it? Every addition to computer infrastructure comes with a risk. Networked printers are extremely helpful to businesses, but hackers have a reputation for gaining access to a network by exploiting vulnerabilities in the printer software. When anything is going to be changed, IT staff must weigh the risk versus the benefit to conclude whether change is a safe idea. After all, adding that Wi-Fi-enabled coffee pot may just give a hacker the entry point they need.

Physical Security

A common theme in cyberpunk novels (a literary subgenre about hackers) involves breaking into a building at night and compromising the network from within. This is a real threat, because any person that has physical access to a computer has a significant advantage when it comes to hacking. Physical security involves restricting actual bodily access to parts of a building or locking doors so a hacker doesn't have the chance to slip by and walk off with an HDD.

Operations

Many, many notable hacks were performed by employees of the organization that had too many access permissions. Using the information and access that they are granted, these hackers commit an "inside job" and make off with their goals. Security teams attempt to prevent this by only giving just enough access to everyone that they need to do their job. It just goes to show, security staff cannot even trust their coworkers.

These are not all of the CISSP domains, but they are the most notable. Interestingly, the domains give an insight into the methodology and philosophy that security IT have when protecting data, and how hackers have to be wary of exactly how CISSPs operate.

The most useful knowledge about modern security for hackers, though, is an intimate idea of how businesses conduct operations. Understanding that most businesses store data on a server and authenticate themselves through Windows domains is a decent first step, but real-world experience is needed to actually understand what makes computer infrastructure tick.

Chapter 3: Common Terms

One important aspect of hacking involves a deep understanding of a multitude of computing concepts. In this chapter, we will broadly cover a few important ones.

Programming

The skill of writing instructional code for a computer is known as programming. Original programming was done with only binary 1s and 0s. Programming nowadays is done with high-level programming languages that are decently close to plain English with special characters mixed in. Programs must be compiled, which means translated into machine code before they can run. Understanding the basics of programming gives a hacker much insight into how the applications they are trying to exploit work, which might just give them an edge.

Algorithms

Algorithms are repeated tasks that lead to a result. For example, multiplication problems can be solved through an algorithm that repeatedly adds numbers. 5 x 3 is the same as 5 + 5 + 5. Algorithms are the basis of encryption- repeated scrambling is done to data to obfuscate it.

Cryptography

Cryptography is the study and practice of encryption and decryption. Encrypting a file involves scrambling the data contents around through a variety of algorithms. The more complex the algorithm, the harder the encryption is to reverse, or decrypt. Important files are almost always encrypted so they cannot be read without the password that begins the decryption. Encryption can be undone through various other means, too, such as cryptoanalysis (intense evaluation and study of data patterns that might lead to discovering the password) or attacks.

Passwords

Passwords are a key phrases that authenticates a user to access information not usually accessible to those not authorized. We use passwords for just about everything in computers, and cracking passwords is a prize for most hackers. Passwords can be compromised many different ways, but mostly through database leaks, social engineering, or weak passwords.

Hardware

The physical components of a computer that make them work. Here's a small security tidbit: the US government is sometimes worried that hardware coming from China is engineered in such a way that would allow China to hack into US government computers.

Software

Software is any program of written code that performs a task. Software examples range from word processors to web browsers to operating systems. Software can also be referred to as programs, applications, and apps.

Scripts

A small piece of code that achieves a simple task can be called a script. Usually not a full-fledged program or software because it is just too small.

Operating Systems

The large piece of software on a computer that is used as a framework for other smaller applications is called an operating system or OS. Most computers run a variant of

Microsoft operating systems, but some use Apple OSX or GNU+Linux-based operating systems.

Linux

Simply put, Linux is a kernel (kernel = underlying OS code) that facilitates complex operating systems. While Windows uses the NT kernel as a core, operating systems such as Ubuntu and Debian use the Linux kernel as a core. Linux operating systems are very different from the ones we are used to, because they do not run .exe files or have a familiar interface. In fact, some Linux operating systems are purely text-based. Linux, though, is very powerful to a hacker because it can run software that Windows cannot, and some of this software is designed with security and hacking specifically in mind. We will see in later chapters how Linux can be used to our advantage.

Computer Viruses

A broad term that usually encompasses a variety of threats. It can mean virus, worm, Trojan, malware, or any other malicious piece of software. Specifically, a virus in particular is a self-replicating harmful program. Viruses copy themselves to other computers and continue to infect like the common cold. Some viruses are meant to annoy the user, others are meant to destroy a system, and some even hide and cause unseen damage behind the scenes. Strange computer activity or general slowness can sometimes be a virus.

Worms

Worms are malicious pieces of code that do not need a host computer. Worms "crawl" through networks and have far reaching infections.

Trojans

Named from the ancient "Trojan Horse", Trojans are bad software that are disguised as helpful programs. If you've ever got an infection from downloading a program on the internet, then you were hit by a Trojan. Trojans are often bundled in software installations and copied alongside actually helpful programs.

Malware

Malware is a general and generic term for mischievous programs, such as scripts, ransomware, and all those mentioned above.

Ransomware

Ransomware is a specific type of malware that cleverly encrypts user's files and demands payment for the decryption password. Highly effective, as large businesses that require their data be always available (hospitals, schools, etc...) usually have to pay the fee to continue business.

Botnet

Worms and other types of malware sometimes infect computers with a larger purpose. Botnets are interconnected networks of infected computers that respond to a hacker's bidding. Infected "zombies" can be made to run as a group and pool resources for massive DDoS attacks that shut down corporate and government websites. Some botnet groups use the massive combined computing power to brute-force passwords and decrypt data. Being part of a malicious botnet is never beneficial.

Proxy

There exist helpful tools for hackers and individuals concerned with privacy. Proxies are services that route your internet content to another place as to hide your true location. For example, if you were to post online though a proxy located in Sweden, the post would look as though it was initially created in Sweden, rather than where you actually live. Hackers use proxies to hide their true location should they ever be found out. Security-concerned people use proxies to throw off obtrusive surveillance.

VPN

A Virtual Private Network is a service/program that "tunnels" internet traffic. It works very much like a proxy, but can hide various other information in addition to encryption of the internet packets. VPNs are typically used by business employees that work away from the office. An employee can connect to their VPN and they will be tunneled through to the corporate server and can access data as if they were sitting in an office work chair. VPNs can be used by hackers to hide location and data information, or to create a direct link to their target. A VPN link to an office server will certainly give more privilege than an average internet connection would.

Penetration Testing

Penetration testing, or pen testing, is the benevolent act of searching for vulnerabilities in security that a hacker might use to their advantage. Security experts can do pen testing as a full time job and get paid by companies to discover exploits before the "bad guys" do.

Vulnerability

An exploit or problem within a program or network that can be used to gain extra access is referred to as a vulnerability. An exploit in the popular Sony video game console Playstation 3 let hackers install pirated games for free instead of paying for them. Finding an exploit or vulnerability is another large goal for hackers.

Bug

A glitch or problem within a program that produces unexpected results. Bugs can sometimes be used to make an exploit, so hackers are always checking for bugs in program, and security experts are always trying to resolve bugs.

Internet

The internet is a network of connected computers that can communicate with each other. Websites are available by communicating with web servers, and games can be played after connecting to a game server. Ultimately every computer on the internet can be communicated with by every other computer depending on the computer's security settings.

Intranet

By comparison, an INTRAnet is a local network consisting of only a few computers. Companies might use intranets to share files securely and without putting them through the entire internet where they could be intercepted. VPNs are usually used to connect to private intranets.

IP

An IP (Internet Protocol) address is the numerical identifier given to a device on a network. Every computer on the internet has a public IP, which is the IP that can geographically pinpoint a computer. We use IP addresses to connect to websites, but instead of typing a number such as 192.168.1.0, we type the domain name (google.com) which uses a DNS server to translate into the numerical IP.

You can learn your local/private IP address by typing *ipconfig* into a Windows command prompt. Some websites, such as http://whatismyipaddress.com/ can reveal your public IP address.

```
C:\windows\system32\cmd.exe

Windows IP Configuration

Ethernet adapter Local Area Connection:

   Connection-specific DNS Suffix  . :
   Link-local IPv6 Address . . . . . :
   IPv4 Address. . . . . . . . . . . : 10.1.15.33
   Subnet Mask . . . . . . . . . . . : 255.255.0.0
   Default Gateway . . . . . . . . . : 10.1.1.2
```

That was a ton of vocab words wasn't it? Take a break! If you've liked what you've read and love the information you're getting, I humbly ask you to leave an honest review for my book! If you're ready, go on to chapter 4.

Chapter 4: Getting Started Hacking

Firstly, this book assumes that the aspiring hacker is using a Windows-based operating system. One of the best tools available on Windows is the command prompt, which can be accessed by following these directions:

1. Press and hold the windows button and the "r" key. This brings up "Run".

2. In the "Open:" field, type "cmd" and click okay.

3. The command prompt will open as a black terminal with white text.

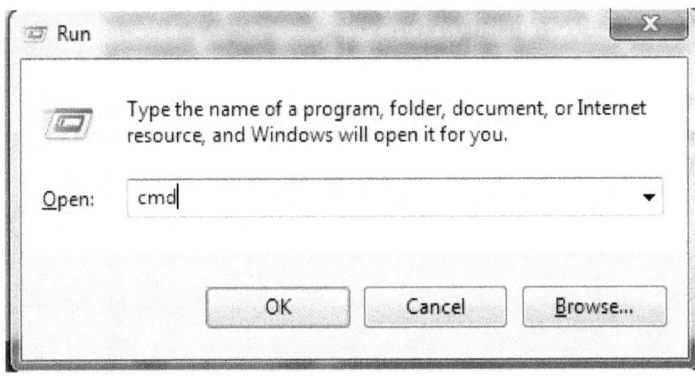

The command prompt resembles old DOS prompts or Linux terminals in aesthetics and functionality. Essentially, the entire computer can be interfaced through the command prompt without ever using a mouse, and this is how older computers worked! It is an essential tool for hackers because there are commands and hacking methods that are only possible through typing commands into the prompt.

$C:\backslash Users\backslash name\backslash >$

is the current directory (folder) in which you are located. You can type "*dir*" and press enter to view the contents of the directory. To change folders, you would type "*cd foldername*". You can also go backwards by typing "*cd ..*". More commands can be viewed by typing "*help*". It is strongly encouraged that the aspiring hacker learn and master the command line, because cmd is a hacker's best friend!

Hacking is a broad term to describe a variety of methods to achieve an end goal of gaining access to a system. Although some hackers do it for fun, others do it for personal gain. No matter how it is achieved, it must come about through a variety of technical methods, which will be described below. A few might have a demonstration attached to them; feel free to start your hacking career by following along.

Social Engineering

Social engineering is a hacking technique that doesn't actually involve technical skill. In this method, an attacker gains access to information "socially".

Here is a story as an example. A clever hacker finds out that a certain employee of a company has a broken computer that they sent to IT to repair. The hacker calls the employee impersonating a new IT member and says that they are nearly finished with the repair, but they need her password to continue. If the disguise works, the employee will freely give over her password and the hacker is successful. Social engineering is extremely popular due to the trusting nature of people and cunning tricks that hackers have gained through experience.

Phishing

Phishing is a type of social engineering involving moderate technical skill. Derived from fishing, phishing is the act of "luring" employees to give information through email. Phishing can employ malware to accomplish its goal as well. Another story follows.

An accountant in the business office has finished payroll for the week, and they check their email to find an unread message. The subject: "URGENT: PAYROLL DECLINED" catches the accountant's attention. The email comes from payroll@adponline1.com, which the accountant has never seen before, but then again this problem has never happened previously so they do not know what to expect. "Your time clock readings did not come through correctly due to an authorization error. Please reply with your password for confirmation" reads the body. The clock reads 4:57, and everyone is about to go home, so the accountant is eager to get along with their day. Replying to the message with their password, the employee goes home, not realizing they just gave their password away to a hacker who now has access to payroll information.

Phishing is highly effective and usually the initial cause of data breaches. This fact comes about because of the general believability of phishing emails, which often use personal information to look legitimate. Additionally, most employees are not computer savvy enough to understand the difference between a fake password request and a real one.

Recently, many companies have begun allocating funds to security training programs for employees. These courses specifically teach how to guard against phishing attempts. Despite this, the brightest hackers will always be able to con and socially engineer their way into sensitive information.

DoS

Denial of Service (DoS) is an attack where multiple network requests are sent to a website or server in order to overload and crash it. DoS attacks can bring down infrastructure not prepared to handle large volumes of requests all at once. A few hackers use DoS attacks as a distraction or added nuisance to cover up their actual attack as it happens. Hackers can send individual network requests through the Windows command prompt as seen below:

```
C:\windows\system32\cmd.exe

Microsoft Windows [Version 6.1.7601]
Copyright (c) 2009 Microsoft Corporation. All rights reserved.

C:\Users\        >ping google.com

Pinging google.com [216.58.217.238] with 32 bytes of data:
Reply from 216.58.217.238: bytes=32 time=21ms TTL=54
Reply from 216.58.217.238: bytes=32 time=49ms TTL=54
Reply from 216.58.217.238: bytes=32 time=21ms TTL=54
Reply from 216.58.217.238: bytes=32 time=20ms TTL=54

Ping statistics for 216.58.217.238:
    Packets: Sent = 4, Received = 4, Lost = 0 (0% loss),
Approximate round trip times in milli-seconds:
    Minimum = 20ms, Maximum = 49ms, Average = 27ms

C:\Users\        >_
```

Here, just a few bytes of data are being sent to google.com, but you can specify how many by altering the command like so:

ping –f –l 65500 websitename

The "*-f*" makes sure the packet is not fragmented or broken up, and "*-l*" lets you input a packet size from 32-65500, thereby increasing the size of the packet and the number of resources it consumes.

Now certainly the average hacker will never be able to take down a website such as google.com through ping requests on command prompt, so the above is for educational purposes only- real DoS attacks involve a powerful computer spamming the network with requests until the server slows to a crawl or crashes outright.

Anti-hackers respond to a high volume of traffic coming from a single origin by blocking that IP from making further requests. They can also observe the type of traffic flooding the server and block packet-types that look like DoS spam.

DDoS

Much more dangerous, DDoS (distributed denial of service) attacks are exponentially stronger than simple denial of service attacks. DDoS attacks involve attacking a server with multiple DoS attacks concurrently, each originating from various different locations. These attacks are much harder to block, because the original IP addresses are constantly changing, or there are just too many to block effectively.

      One example of how devastating DDoS attacks can be came from the Sony attack of December 2014. Sony's newest game console (at the time) had just come out, and kids were opening them on Christmas day anxious to begin having fun. After hooking them up to the internet though, the disappointed kids were met with error messages stating that the Sony Network was down. The hacker collective Lizard Squad had been DDoSing Sony and overloading their game servers just for fun. Additionally, millions of new players were trying to access the service to play games and inquire about the down-time as well, which flooded the infrastructure even more. This created an issue for Sony, as they could not just block all requests because some were legitimate customers. The issue was finally resolved when the DDoSing was stopped, but the situation proved just how easily a coordinated network attack can cripple large servers.

      Security Professionals have a few tools to prevent DDoS attacks from occurring. Load balancing hardware can spread out large requests among various servers, as to not bog down a single machine. They can also block the main sources of the attacks, pinging and DNS requests. Some companies, such as CloudFlare, offer web software that can actively identify and emergently block any traffic it believes is a DDoS attempt.

Performing DDoS attacks is relatively easy. Open-source software exists by the name of LOIC (Low Orbit Ion Cannon) that allows ease-of-use for DDoSing. The software can be seen below:

Rather humorous, the childish gui hides powerful tools that allow unskilled, beginner hackers to have DDoS capabilities when coordinating with others.

The most skilled attackers use botnets to increase their effectiveness. A well-written worm can infect data centers or universities with fast internet connections, and then these zombie computers all coordinate under the will of the hacker to attack a single target.

Fork Bomb

Fork bombs are a specific type of malicious code that works essentially like an offline DDoS. Instead of clogging network pipes, though, fork bombs clog processing pipes. Basically, a fork bomb is a process that runs itself recursively- that is the process copies itself over and over until the processor of a computer cannot keep up. If a hacker has access to a system and can run code, fork bombs are fairly deadly. Actually, fork bombs are one of the simplest programs to write. Typing "start" into a command prompt will open up another command prompt. This can be automated as demonstrated and pictured below.

1. Open notepad. (Windows+R, notepad, okay)

2. Type "start forkbomb.bat" as the first and only line.

3. Open the "save as" dialog.

4. Switch the file-type to "all files".

5. Name the file "forkbomb.bat", and then save the file.

What we have just done is create a batch file in the same programming language that command prompt uses. Running this file (by right clicking its icon and then clicking "run") initiates the fork bomb, and it will continuously launch itself over and over until the computer cannot handle the resource strain. WARNING: Do not run this file unless you are prepared to face the consequences!

Cracking

Cracking is breaking into software/applications or passwords. Cracks can disable Digital Rights Management (DRM, also known as copy protection) on paid software so that full versions of software can be used without paying the full price. Skillful hackers achieve this by reverse-engineering code or finding exploits that let them run their own code. Encryption can be cracked as well, which leads to protected data being compromised since the attacker knows how to reverse the scrambling. Password cracking can be achieved through brute force cracking and dictionary attacks.

Brute Force

Brute force attacks attempt to guess a password by attempting *every* conceivable combination of letters and numbers. This was not terribly difficult in the days of DOS, where a password could only be 8 characters max. Brute force attacks are long and arduous, but can be successful on a powerful computer given enough time. Later in the chapter, we will talk about Kali Linux and its use as a security testing/hacking tool. Hydra is an application that can attempt to brute force passwords.

Dictionary Attack

Dictionary attacks are slightly more sophisticated. They are similar to brute force attacks in that they try a large combination of passwords, but they differ in the fact that dictionary attacks use a database of words from a dictionary to operate. This method works well at guessing passwords that are simple, such as one-word passwords. The application facilitating the dictionary attack will go through a large database of words starting at the top and try every one with slight variations to see if login is successful. The most clever dictionary attacks add words specific to the user to the database, such as their name, pets, work, birthday, etc... Most people use personal information as a password, and adding this information to a dictionary attack increases effectiveness.

Controlling a Colleague's Screen on Windows

Certain versions of Windows contain the "Remote Desktop" application built in, which is designed for IT personnel to quickly and remotely connect to a faraway computer to control and perform maintenance on it.

Remote desktop can be exploited (of course) and that is what we will do. This tutorial is designed for two computers on the same network, but clever users may be able to expand this to the entire internet.

Firstly, remote desktop needs to be enabled on both computers. Through control panel, click on "System" and then "Remote settings". Ensure "Allow Remote Assistance connections to this computer" is checked. Apply settings. Then, you will need your colleagues IP address; you may recall this can be done by typing *ipconfig* into a command prompt and copying the "IPv4 Address" listed.

Now to initiate the remote control procedure, wait for the right time to surprise your friends and start the "Remote Desktop Connection" application on your computer (you can search for it in the start menu). Type in the friend's IP address and watch their surprised reaction when you move their mouse around!

Not technically a "hack", the remote desktop application CAN be used by hackers to spy on their targets. For example, an unsuspecting user may check bank account information while the hacker watches silently.

This gives the hacker a good idea of passwords and personal information, so be wary if the remote desktop application is enabled on your computer.

Using another OS

Alternate operating systems are invaluable to a hacker for a variety of reasons. An easy way to try another operating system without overwriting the current one is to install the OS onto a bootable USB drive. We will demonstrate this process by installing Kali Linux (formally Backtrack Linux) onto a USB drive.

1. Download Kali Linux by visiting http://www.kali.org . You will need to download the version that is compatible with your processor (32 bit, 64 bit, or ARM). If in doubt, download the .iso file for 32 bit processors.

2. Download Rufus, the free USB writing software from http://rufus.akeo.ie

3. Plug in any USB storage stick with enough space for the Kali image. You might need 8GB or more depending on how big the image is at your time of reading.

4. WARNING: make sure the USB does not contain any valuable files- they will be deleted! Copy anything important off of the drive or you risk losing the data forever.

5. Start Rufus, select your USB stick from in the "Device" tab, and keep the rest of the settings default. Refer to the image below for the settings I have used.

6. Beside the checked "Create a bootable disk using" box, select "ISO Image" from the dropdown. Then click the box beside it and locate the Kali .iso.

7. Triple check that the information is correct, and that your USB has no important files still on it.

8. Click "Start".

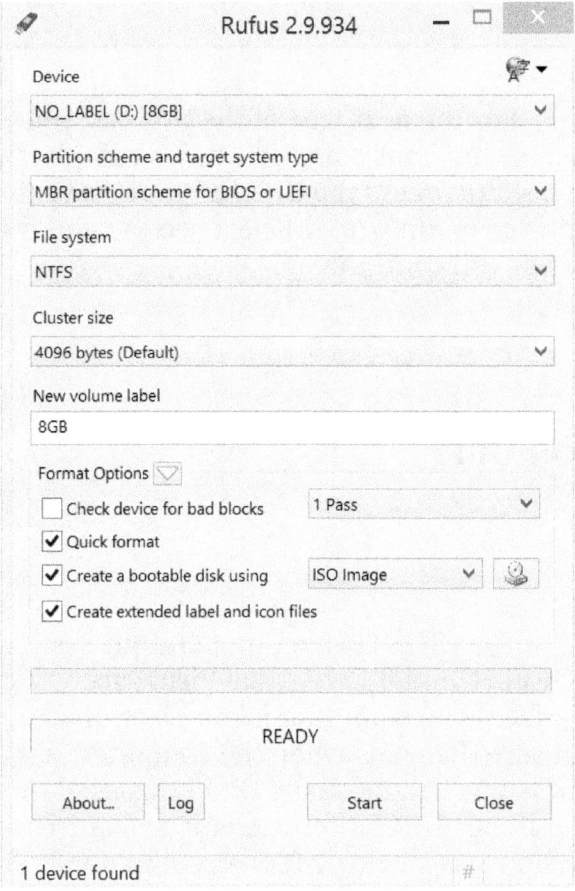

Rufus will take its time to finish. Once Rufus replies with "Done", it will have installed Kali Linux onto the USB and made it bootable.

After finishing completely you are free to close out of the program.

For the next part of the process, you will need to shut your computer down completely. We need to access the BIOS of your computer. Continue reading on the next section and the process will continue.

BIOS/UEFI

The BIOS (Basic Input Output System) or UEFI (Unified Extensible Firmware Interface) of a computer is the piece of firmware that runs when the computer first powers on. Traditionally BIOS was used by default, but UEFI offers enhanced features and it is slowly replacing BIOS on computers. This startup firmware performs initialization, checks hardware, and provides options for the user to interact with their computer on the "bare metal" level. BIOS/UEFI interfaces can be accessed by pressing a key on the keyboard when the computer first starts up. The specific keyboard button needed varies between motherboard manufacturers, so the user needs to pay attention to their screen for the first few moments after powering on. After pressing the button, the computer will not boot into the operating system like normal, rather it will load the interface associated with BIOS/UEFI and give control to the user.

Continuing the demonstration of booting into an OS contained on a USB stick, the user now needs to set USB drives to boot before hard drives. Every motherboard manufacturer will use their own custom interface, so this book cannot explain the specific steps for each motherboard model. Basically, the goal is to find the "boot order", which is the order in which the computer checks for bootable operating systems. Under normal conditions, the computer will boot from the internal hard drive first, which is the probably the operating system you are reading this from now. We need to make sure the computer checks the USB drive for an OS before it checks internally. In the image below the hard drive is checked first, then the CD-ROM Drive is checked. Thirdly any removable devices are checked, but this specific computer would probably only get as far as the internal hard drive before finding the primary OS and booting. To boot into our image on the USB drive, move "Removable Devices" to the top of the list. Finally, ensure that the USB is plugged in, save changes to BIOS/UEFI, and reboot. The computer should begin loading Kali Linux.

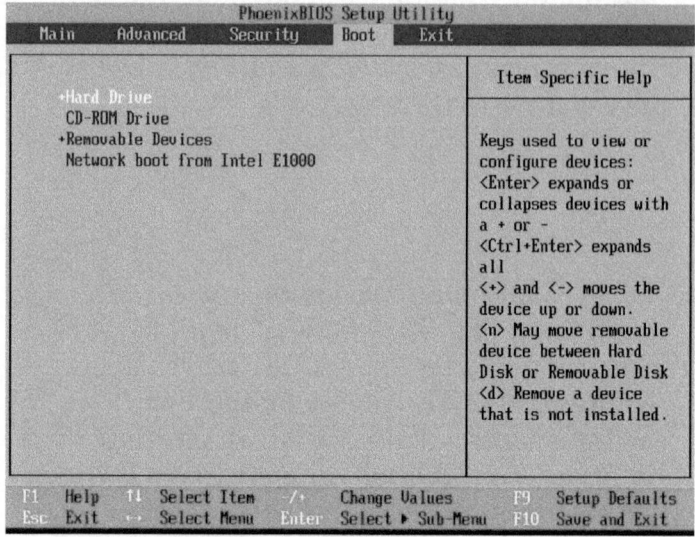

Any problems with booting will give an error message that the user can internet search to troubleshoot, but more than likely the computer will boot into Kali successfully. The user can now use a whole new operating system!

Kali Linux was chosen because of the tools that are available to it by default. Kali is often the go-to OS for hackers due to the software included. Hackers and security professionals alike chose Kali, so it is encouraged that aspiring minds experiment with the OS.

Using another OS to steal data

Here is an interesting point: through the bootable Kali USB you can also load your primary internal hard drive and view the contents. This means that you can access the files on your disk *without booting into Windows*. Try opening up your internal hard drive and viewing your personal files. Sometimes it is shocking to realize how easy it is to view personal data without really turning on Windows. Now admittedly there are a few restrictions on accessing protected data, but this technique can be used to recover secret information from a computer that does not belong to a hacker. Remember, if a computer is accessible physically, hackers have a significant advantage. They could always load up their favorite bootable OS, copy all data in the hard drive, and leave without ever logging into Windows. Even password protected or encrypted data is vulnerable to be copied. Since the attacker has a copy of the locked data, they can spend unlimited time trying to crack the password.

We will take a look at some of the other hacking tools present in Kali Linux below.

Port Scanning

Hacking is made easier with knowledge of the target infrastructure. One of the best ways to map out networks is through port scanning. Scanning ports reveals open points in a network. Having certain ports open can offer unique exploits for hackers, so hackers usually port scan prior to deciding a point-of-entry. On Kali Linux the best tool to do this is nmap. By loading Kali Linux onto a networked computer and running a terminal (Linux version of command prompt, open with ctrl+alt+T), the hacker can enter this command to scan a computer for open ports:

nmap -sV IPADDRESS -A –v

The terminal will run the nmap program with the specified parameters and begin scanning the specified IP address for open ports.

Packet Capture

Traffic through the network is sent as little pieces of data called packets. Each packet contains various bits, such as where it is coming from, where it is going, and whatever information is being sent. An unsecure network might be sending important information as plain, unencrypted text. Data sent this way is open for interception, and that is done through packet capture. Kali Linux has a built in application that does this- Wireshark. Wireshark is also available on Windows, for those that haven't seen the benefits of Kali. Packet capture is done by starting the application, changing your network card's mode to "promiscuous", and starting the packet capture.

Knowledgeable hackers can then view the packets that are captured and study them for information. Plain text will be visible if it is being sent that way, but encrypted text will be obscured.

SQL injection

SQL is a programming language mostly used on web servers; an example of typical code is below. SQL injections exploit poor coding on a website's login script through a clever "injection" of hacker-written code. This is a difficult process to explain, but it can be viewed through YouTube videos and website demos (http://www.codebashing.com/sql_demo).

```
drop table t1
Create table t1 (tim int, rem varchar(100))
select 86400
INSERT INTO t1 VALUES (1251781074, 'day1')
INSERT INTO t1 VALUES (1251781074 + 86400, 'day2')
INSERT INTO t1 VALUES (1251781074 + 2*86400, 'day3')
INSERT INTO t1 VALUES (1251781074 + 3*86400, 'day4')
INSERT INTO t1 VALUES (1251781074 + 4*86400, 'day5')

Select DATEADD(hour,-4,(dateadd(second ,tim, '1/1/1970'))), * From t1

DECLARE @StartDateTime DATETIME
,@EndDateTime DATETIME

SELECT @StartDateTime = '2009-09-02 00:57:54.000'
SELECT @EndDateTime = '2009-09-03 00:57:54.000 '

Select * from t1
Where
 DATEADD(hour,-4,(dateadd(second ,tim, '1/1/1970'))) >= @StartDateTime
AND DATEADD(hour,-4,(dateadd(second ,tim, '1/1/1970'))) <= @EndDateTime
```

Destroying a Linux-based System

Linux-based operating systems are generally more secure than their Windows counterparts, but the design philosophy behind UNIX-like kernels is that superusers (administrators) have total control with no questions asked. Windows administrators generally have full control as well, but the operating system prevents the user from accidentally damaging their system! One very malicious attack involves exploiting the superuser's permissions to delete the entire Linux operating system.

While experimenting with the terminal in Kali Linux, you might have noticed that some commands require "sudo" as a preface. Sudo invokes superuser permissions and allows system-changing commands to run after the root password is input. Since the Linux kernel gives full controls to superusers, entering the following command will completely delete the operating system *even while it is running.*

sudo rm –rf /

Under no circumstance should this command ever be run without permission. This command will break the operating system! Even when testing this command on yourself, be prepared to face the consequences. You cannot blame this guide if something goes wrong. The anatomy of the command is as follows:

Sudo invokes superuser and gives complete control, *rm* signifies remove, *-rf* tells *rm* to remove nested folders and files, and */* starts the deletion process at the very first folder. Thusly the entire system is deleted. If the computer doesn't immediately crash, it certainly will not boot after a shutdown.

Chapter 5: Building Skill and Protecting Oneself

Programming

Learning to code is what separates "script kiddies" from actual elite hackers. Any aspiring hacker should take the time and learn the basics of programming in a variety of languages. A good beginner language is the classic C++. Based on original C, C++ is basic high-level programming language that is powerful and easy enough for first time learners. A variety of books exist on learning the language, and it is recommended for novices.

Programming is an essential skill because most exploits involve using programming code to alter or bypass a system. Viruses and other malware are written with code also, and competent hacker-coders can write awe-inspiring applications such as ransomware.

Mastering Terminal and Command Prompt

Ultimately the terminal is an application that can parse programming code one line at a time. Skillful hackers have mastered moving around the command prompt and terminal. As previously stated, typing *help* into command prompt provides a list of commands. In Linux's bash terminal a user can type *man* (for manual) to learn about commands. Manual pages are long and extremely detailed.

Routers and WEP

Understanding what password protection is used for a Wi-Fi router/access point could potentially help a hacker crack the password. In the early days of Wi-Fi, WEP was used for password security. WEP is an algorithm that lacked complexity and was replaced by WPA in 2004. However, many routers still use WEP by accident or default. This gives hackers a common exploit, because WEP keys are crackable in a short amount of time. To do this on Kali Linux a hacker must start the OS on a laptop with wireless within range of the WEP access point. Then, they would open a terminal and use the airmon-ng application.

Cracking WPA keys is much more time consuming due to the increased complexity, but WEP keys are easy targets for hackers to practice their emerging skills.

Protecting Oneself as a Hacker

Curious hackers that are learning skills mentioned in this book must take care to protect themselves. Any serious infiltration attempt should only be attempted on a network in which the individual has permission to experiment and penetration test. Depending on the state or federal laws of the reader, various police action could be taken against an individual without explicit permission to perform this book's demonstrations; astute hackers would already be wary of this.

All of this aside, it is beneficial for aspiring hackers to learn various methods to keep themselves safe from identification. Additionally, many hacktivists attempting to reveal the illegal activities of the company (whistleblowing) in which they work are monitored constantly. Only through some of the subjects we talk about below are these people safe from the oppressive nature that employers can inflict. General security is not only a decent practice, security can protect those trying to protect others. For hackers, security safeguards against "counter-hacks" and keeps the field advancing.

Password Security

The largest difference between the average computer user and a security expert would be password complexity. While the average employee might use "fido82" for their authentication key, security experts might use something less guessable such as "Fsdf3@3". Sharp hackers will take advantage of this fact when dictionary attacking passwords. Furthermore, some passwords and infrastructures will be too well-protected for any beginner to break. As skill increases, hackers become wiser. Sage-like hackers can produce new exploits seemingly out of thin-air, and it is assured that any person can achieve this level with enough practice.

With self-introspection, attackers and hactivists alike must live up to the standards that security experts live by. A strong personal password will nearly guarantee that a hacker cannot be "counter-hacked". As we will read in the next few sections, most hackers are persecuted because their devices are seized and easily counter-hacked to reveal nefarious activity. Complex passwords will stand up to the robust supercomputers of federal governments.

It is also recommended to never write passwords down or save them to a file somewhere. The best passwords are random, memorized, and secret.

Password Leaks

Furthermore, security experts will rarely repeat passwords. Shockingly, plenty of users do just that- the average person uses the same password for banking, social media, forums, and online shopping! 2015's Ashley Madison leak saw the online publication of email addresses; 2013's Tumblr leak had passwords going up for sale on the "darknet" (black market internet). Since users rarely change passwords, savvy hackers can search these databases and locate user information. The passwords have most likely stayed the same, so the hacker has effortlessly gained access to an account. Password leaks are common and readily searchable on the internet too, just access https://haveibeenpwned.com/ to check if a password is compromised! Conclusively, these leaks do not hurt users that change passwords regularly and keep them different for each account.

Encryption

Encryption is available to Windows users that are on a Professional/Enterprise version by default. Otherwise, a user wishing to encrypt files will have to download a 3rd party application such as TrueCrypt (http://www.truecrypt.org). Encryption is essential for users wishing to protect any kind of data. Whether it is bad poetry, trade secrets, or a log of successful hacks, the files need to be encrypted if you want to guarantee that absolutely nobody should be able to read it. Snoopy roommates will therefore not be able to access the contents of the file without your expressed permission, and law enforcement officials that seize a computer reach a dead end when greeted with the prompt for a decryption password.

The process is done on Windows by right clicking a file, accessing the properties, clicking the advanced properties button in the "Attributes" section, then checking the "Encrypt contents to secure data" checkbox. A screenshot is visible below:

Every tip previously offered about passwords applies when choosing a decryption key. It is essential to remember that if a beginner hacker could break the encryption, then certainly the combined intelligence power of a government could crack the key as well.

History

Although obvious, not many novices realize that computer history can compromise an operation. For the uninitiated, browser history is a log of visited websites that is stored on a computer. This list if often not encrypted, so a compromised list with "how to hack" on recent searches could be incriminating evidence when brought before a court. Most computer users disable browser history altogether for privacy reasons, and the process is not difficult. In Firefox, for example, the option is found under the "Privacy" tab of "Options". Disabling history is useful, but clearing out previous history might be needed as well. Once again the methodology varies, but the general process is to access the list of recently viewed websites and clear it through a button or command.

History is not always exclusively stored locally. Some ISPs (Internet Service Providers, the organizations that provide users with internet access) keep their own log of internet history. Police subpoenas would require them to hand over this history, which basically voids the care put into deleting internet history. There are ways around this fact however, which will be explicated in the following sections.

Using a Proxy

The reason that ISPs know internet history is related to how hackers intercept packets to view information. Regular, unencrypted webpage traffic is predicable in how it looks and can therefore be captured. Internet service providers sometimes keep this information by habit or law, so the only way to remove this annoyance is to disguise the data packets as something else entirely. Proxies allow users to do this. Normal packets will have the source and destination address clearly marked, while a packet sent through a proxy will not show the initial sender, only the proxy machine that relayed the packets. On the ISP's end, it seems as though the computer is communicating with one address while they are really communicating with another. When a court subpoenas the ISP for information, there is no link between the source (hacker) and the ultimate destination (target).

Proxies can be used through a web browser (hide.me, whoer.net, proxysite.com, etc...) or as a 3rd party piece of software. Proxies are most famously used in college networks to evade content filtering- nobody can block your gaming websites if it looks like you are connecting to something else entirely.

Proxies do have their downsides, though. Law agencies with enough power can retrieve records from a proxy server and match up "timestamps" of your connections to piece together your internet history. Using multiple proxies only delays the inevitable, because if detectives have one proxy server compromised then they can just keep tracing them from proxy to proxy until the origin address is reached.

Using a VPN

Earlier in the book VPNs were explained to "tunnel" data through a network. This service is usually used by employees to work from home, but hackers can exploit VPNs to work as an enhanced proxy of sorts. A typical VPN alters packets in such a way as to encrypt them and make them unreadable. The packets will not look like web activity, because they are sent through a different port entirely. This adds a layer of complexity to the packets that suits their use for security. For example, a public, open network is dangerous to check your bank statements on, because the packets can be readily intercepted and decoded by hackers. Using a VPN, though, hides the data and allows normal, unrestricted use that is not in danger of being decrypted.

Competent hackers will use the proxy-like qualities of a VPN to hide their true location. Usually these servers are moderately more secure from government agencies as well due to the added obscurity and difficulty of determining origin points. Internet pirates are quite fond of virtual private networks because they can conceal the illegal data they download as regular, protected data.

VPNs are usually created through 3rd party software. The program OpenVPN allows anybody to connect to a VPN server, but they will most likely need a username and password. Organizations typically have private VPNs that act as relays only to company intranets, and these relays need company provided passwords. Individuals that wish to use a VPN might have to pay money for the ability to connect to a VPN server, but hackers agree VPNs are money well spent.

Tor Project

For hackers and security experts seeking the highest level of protection, the Tor Project (http://torproject.org) offers a solution. The company offers a piece of free software called Tor, which acts as a super-VPN/proxy. Tor bounces internet traffic across thousands of relays (each with substantial encryption) to ensure that the destination and origin of the packets are not clear. This software can be used by any individual wishing to hide their online activities, and it has proved decently effective.

Browser Fingerprint

Somewhat of an advanced topic, browser fingerprinting is an elaborate anti-hacking technique where specific unique information contained in your web browser (language packs, ad-ons, OS version, etc...) is retained by websites and used to identify users.

Most hackers use unique configurations with adblocking plugins, IP obscuring software, and other defining characteristics. The irony of this is that the uniqueness gained from protecting oneself becomes an identifying factor through device fingerprinting.

Basically, the best way to stay hidden on the internet is to "blend in" with the crowd, so a unique configuration cannot be traced back to a hacker. Since this is such an advanced and emerging topic, it is too early to say whether detectives and cyber investigators are catching criminals with this methodology. A browser fingerprint can be viewed through online testers, such as https://amiunique.org.

Open Source vs. Proprietary

Throughout this book some software has been referred to as "free". The actual correct term for the software is FOSS (free and open source software). Programs that are FOSS are not only monetarily free, they are also transparent in their coding. Open-source refers to the fact that the coding of the program is visible at any time, whereas proprietary software's code is not visible ever. This fact is important; if code is not visible, there is no way to know exactly what the program is doing or who it is sending data to. Proprietary software, such as Google's web browser Chrome, unquestionably sends data back to Google. Contrasting starkly is Mozilla's FOSS Firefox web browser. Firefox has transparent code, so at any time programmers can read through the source and know for certain whether Firefox sends data back.

Hackers and security-minded people tend to gravitate towards FOSS because of its more safe nature. After all, nobody knows exactly what is going on under the hood of some dubious proprietary programs. There might exist backdoors for governments that would expose good-natured hackers or whistleblowers within closed-source software, so the best security is always done through well maintained free and open source software.

Throwaways

Whistleblowers and other high level leakers (see: Edward Snowden) require the utmost privacy with zero chance of linking an action to a person. Many professionals decide to do their private doings through throwaway devices.

A throwaway is a computer that is only used for the private doings. It is usually bought with cash, has no mention of the buyer's name, is never used to log into accounts associated with the buyer, and is used in a public place such as a coffee shop. If used correctly, there should not be a single shred of evidence pointing back to the buyer.

It is important that throwaways be bought with cash because a bill of sale with a name on it is an undeniable link. It is for these reasons that hackers rarely, if ever, use credit cards for purchases. Cash is virtually untraceable, but security cameras can still pick out a face in a store. Buying used or from yard sales removes any monitoring capabilities an organization might have had.

Signing into personal accounts leaves traces on the device, and using personal internet connections will lead back to the IP registered to you by the ISP. Coffee Shops, McDonalds, libraries, and internet cafes usually offer free internet without signing up- these places are the locations of choice for anonymity.

Bitcoin

If something must be bought online, bitcoin is an anonymous way to do so. Bitcoin is a virtual currency that isn't attached to a name. Criminals in the past have used bitcoin to purchase illegal substances on the "darknet", which proves how anonymous bitcoin can be.

Conclusion

The demonstrations in this book are admittedly basic, for they were provided to stimulate an interest in security/hacking. Hackers must cultivate their skill through practice and studying. To gain skill, you must study networking basics, security concepts, programming languages, cryptography, and much more. Endurance and tenacity mold the brightest into outstanding hackers, so lifelong learning should be an aspiration for any hacker. Your journey continues with great hope and promise.

Thank you again for downloading this book!

I hope this book was able to help you to understand some of the core concepts revolving around security, hacking, and counter-hacking. The scope of the subject is so large that this book could not ever hope to cover everything. Even though the time spent on various subjects in this book was brief, I encourage you to research them further.

Remember that security and hacking are relevant today more than ever. This book encourages curious minds to inspire to adhere to the "hacker's manifesto" and be guilty of no crime save curiosity. This book does not encourage illegal activity, it encourages exploration and entertainment.

Finally, if you enjoyed this book, please take the time to share your thoughts and post a review on Amazon. It'd be greatly appreciated!

Thank you and good luck!

Hacking University: Junior Edition. Learn Python Computer Programming from Scratch

Become a Python Zero to Hero. The Ultimate Beginners Guide in Mastering the Python Language

BY: ISAAC D. CODY

HACKING UNIVERSITY

JUNIOR EDITION

Learn Python Computer Programming from Scratch

Become a Python Zero to Hero. The Ultimate Beginners Guide in Mastering the Python Language

ISAAC D. CODY

Table of Contents

Introduction

Related Software

Online Resources

The Job Market

History of Python

Why Use Python?

Benefits of Python

Setting up a Development Environment

Hello World

Programming Concepts

Variables

Variable Types

Input

String Formatting

Example Program 1

Decision Structures

Conditional Operators

Example Program 2

Loops

Example Program 3

More about Variables

Example Program 4

Functions

Example Program 5

Classes

Special Methods

Example Program 6

Inheritance

[Example Program 7](#)

[Modules](#)

[Example Program 8](#)

[Common Errors](#)

[Conclusion](#)

[Related Titles](#)

Copyright 2016 by <u>Isaac D. Cody</u> - All rights reserved.

This document is geared towards providing exact and reliable information in regards to the topic and issue covered. The publication is sold with the idea that the publisher is not required to render accounting, officially permitted, or otherwise, qualified services. If advice is necessary, legal or professional, a practiced individual in the profession should be ordered.

- From a Declaration of Principles which was accepted and approved equally by a Committee of the American Bar Association and a Committee of Publishers and Associations.

In no way is it legal to reproduce, duplicate, or transmit any part of this document in either electronic means or in printed format. Recording of this publication is strictly prohibited and any storage of this document is not allowed unless with written permission from the publisher. All rights reserved.

The information provided herein is stated to be truthful and consistent, in that any liability, in terms of inattention or otherwise, by any usage or abuse of any policies, processes, or directions contained within is the solitary and utter responsibility of the recipient reader.

Under no circumstances will any legal responsibility or blame be held against the publisher for any reparation, damages, or monetary loss due to the information herein, either directly or indirectly.

Respective authors own all copyrights not held by the publisher.

The information herein is offered for informational purposes solely, and is universal as so. The presentation of the information is without contract or any type of guarantee assurance.

The trademarks that are used are without any consent, and the publication of the trademark is without permission or backing by the trademark owner. All trademarks and brands within this book are for clarifying purposes only and are the owned by the owners themselves, not affiliated with this document.

Disclaimer

All rights reserved. No part of this publication may be reproduced, distributed, or transmitted in any form or by any means, including photocopying, recording, or other electronic or mechanical methods, without the prior written permission of the publisher, except in the case of brief quotations embodied in critical reviews and certain other noncommercial uses permitted by copyright law.

Introduction

Thank you for downloading the book *"Hacking University: Junior Edition. Learn Python Computer Programming from Scratch. Become a Python Zero to Hero. The Ultimate Beginners Guide in Mastering the Python Language."*

Python is a powerful and highly recommended language for beginners for a variety of reasons. This book serves as a beginners guide for those that have never written programming code before, so even if the thought of programming is daunting this book can explain it in simple terms. We will introduce the process from the very beginning with actual code examples; follow along to learn a valuable computer skill that can potentially land you a job working with the elegant Python language.

Related Software

For enhancing your Python skill, use an IDE. If you have not downloaded it yet, Atom is highly recommended for Python programming. Atom is customizable, in that you can install add-ons at any time to make programming easier. "autocomplete-python" is one such add-on that can guess what you are typing and automatically fill in the rest of the command.

VI and Emacs are two other popular text editors for programmers. Both are considered highly advanced and optimized for writing code, but a bit of a "flame war" exists between fans of both softwares. For the Linux Python programmer, investigate the two text editors and test whether it helps with Python workflow.

After you have finished a particularly useful Python program and wish to distribute it to users, you have to keep in mind that many of them do not have Python installed and will likely not want to install it just to run your program. PyInstaller (http://www.pyinstaller.org/) is a piece of software that builds your Python script and the needed modules into an .exe file that does not need Python to run. It is a handy software should distribute your applications.

Online Resources

For obtaining online help related to Python, you can always check the online documentation (https://www.python.org/doc/). The documentation contains examples and manual pages for every function built-in to Python and its included modules.

For times when programming code just does not work, you can always turn to search engines to resolve your problem. Typing in the error text into Google can turn up other programmers who also had the same problem and posted online. If the problem cannot be fixed by observing other code, websites such as Stack Overflow (http://stackoverflow.com/) are notoriously helpful in resolving code issues. Make an account their and post your problem politely and somebody will probably help you out.

Finally, there are websites that offer tutorials online about how to learn intermediate and advanced Python programming. http://www.learnpython.org/ is one particularly exemplary one, but the sheer amount comes from the fact that Python is highly used and well understood. For any time Python help is needed, a quick internet search may solve your curiosities.

The Job Market

As a popular language and because of its widely implemented use, Python jobs are abundant. Large companies and start-ups alike are looking for programmers that understand Python, and because Python is still increasing in use the jobs prospects will continue to increase.

Most companies do not require college education for programming jobs, because they understand that most programmers are self-taught. Obtaining a job in the Python job market is not difficult because of this, but it still requires preparation and dedication on the programmer's part. Younger Python programmers can gain internships at Google, Apple, Intel, and more just by showing a drive to learn. Adult Python programmers can apply for programming jobs by directly contacting companies or replying to job listings.

Search online in message boards, job sites, and freelance websites such as UpWork for prospects. Also ask around programming groups and attend job fairs to learn about companies that are hiring Python programmers.

Build a decent résumé and be prepared to prove your knowledge with the language. The interview process for programming jobs often contain "whiteboard" programming tests where you are presented with a situation and asked to use Python to solve the issue. They will not be too terribly difficult, but you certainly need to have a decent grasp on Python to pass.

Overall, finding a Python job is easy because of the current market, but also difficult because you need to know Python intimately. Dedicate yourself to applying for as many positions as possible and eventually a job will appear.

History of Python

Python is a programming language with origins in the late 1980's. Guido van Rossum, the creator, was looking to develop a language as a hobby project to supersede the ABC programming language. Taking cues from the popular C language, Python was created to be a powerful but easy to understand scripting language.

The term "scripting language" refers to the fact that written code is not actually compiled, but rather it is interpreted by an application. Normally this means that scripting languages are not nearly as powerful as actual programming languages. For Python, though, the opposite is true- the language remains one of the most powerful available for web servers and desktop clients. Development of Python continued throughout the 1990's until version 2 was released in 2000. The interpreter behind Python became intricate enough that current versions of Python are almost indistinguishable from lower level programming languages.

      Throughout the mid 2000's and even now, Python continues to be developed by Guido van Rossum and a team of dedicated volunteers. The language gained great popularity due to its many benefits, and popular websites such as YouTube, Reddit, and Instagram even use Python for functionality. It seems as though Python will continue to grow for many more years as companies adopt the easy to use but highly useful Python language.

Why Use Python?

When first starting out learning how to program, the huge amount of options, information, and advice can be truly intimidating. Some experts claim that the difficult but time-honored C language is the best start, but other professionals say starting on an easier language such as Java or Python will give the learner a chance to actually absorb key concepts. Python is recommended for this exact reason- programming will not be as foreign and confusing by starting with a straightforward scripting language.

Python is easy to understand, an elegant and clean language, and free of many of the complicated symbols and markings that are used elsewhere. Often accomplishing a task using Python only requires a few lines of neatly formatted code.

Large companies such as Google, Disney, NASA, and Yahoo all use Python for their own programs; having Python knowledge could potentially land a programmer a job working at a high-profile organization. Moreover, because Python is continuously developed today with new features always being added, interest in the language will continuously increase with time. More companies will discover that Python is an exceedingly useful programming language, so learning it now will prepare you for the future.

Benefits of Python

In addition to being easy and fast, Python also has various other benefits. Python is very portable, meaning that Python code can run on a variety of different operating systems. Windows, Mac OSX and Linux distributions are all supported directly, and code written on one platform can be used on all of them.

Power is not compromised by Python's ease-of-use. The interpreter behind the scripting language is able to turn near-natural English commands into low-level processor instructions that put it on par with actual programming languages. Big-name companies choose to use Python because of this, and as websites such as YouTube and Pinterest prove, Python has a wide range of functionality.

Python is clean and retains a focus on readable code. Style and formatting are usually left up to individual programmers, but with Python neatness is absolutely required. For beginner programmers this instills good programming practices, which will dually help with Python and any other languages the novice wishes to learn.

Ease of development and testing also propel Python above other similar languages. Code can be run instantly with the interpreter which allows for rapid prototyping. Being able to quickly test out code means that bugs can be fixed quickly, allowing more time for other development goals.

Conclusively, Python is the perfect language for beginners. Both simple to develop for and learn, Python is also decently powerful. Fantastic for newcomers and those just starting out programming, Python remains the top choice of technology companies everywhere. Learning the language will prove to be useful now and into the future as its popularity continues to grow.

Setting up a Development Environment

Programming languages are typically used on Linux-based operating systems such as Ubuntu and Debian. Python is no exception, but there is another option of developing on Windows. This book will explain how to get both set up. It is important to know though, that we will develop with Python 3, rather than the older (but still extremely popular) Python 2.7.

Most Linux distributions actually come with Python installed by default. Therefore, there are no extra setup procedures to obtaining a working environment. The Python interpreter can be entered by typing "python" into a terminal console. If there are multiple versions installed, though, "python" will start the first one found. Check the version number in the interpreter, and if 2.7 launches you might have to type "python3" into the terminal instead. Press ctlr+c to quit out of the interpreter at any time.

Windows computers usually never have Python preinstalled. To obtain the software, navigate to the [Python website](#) and download the most recent version. As of now, Python 3.5.2 is the current version. So long as your version number is Python 3, the code written in this book should also be compatible. Install the software with mostly default settings. Definitely check the "Add Python to the Path", because it simplifies testing programs. After the installer is done the Python interpreter can be started by searching for "python" in the start menu.

The interpreter, or parser, is one of Python's advertised features that allows for individual lines to be written and run. For testing out code the parser is fantastic, but mostly every program we write in this book will be multiline, so we will need an IDE (integrated Development Environment). Windows has a few popular solutions, such as Atom, Pycharm, and Eclipse. These are all 3rd party applications that can be downloaded and installed. IDEs are essentially glorified text editors that offer helpful programming features such as syntax highlighting and command-completion. Although Atom is highly recommended for Windows developers, Python comes with an IDE solution already. IDLE is an interpreter program that can be made multiline by clicking on "file" and then "new file". Whether you choose to use the preinstalled editor or choose to get a full-fledged programming environment through Atom/Eclipse, the Python code will work just the same. You will write your code within one of the multiline programs.

On Linux you also have the option of downloading a Python-compatible IDE application, but most programmers tend to use the preinstalled application "nano". Nano is a built-in, barebones text editor accessible by typing "nano" into a console. The program can actually do some rudimentary syntax highlighting once it knows a Python script is being written, so many developers prefer the basic setup provided. Code is written into nano, then saved by pressing ctrl+x.

Now that there is a development environment set up, you can continue onwards to begin writing your first Python program.

Hello World

Mostly every programmer gets introduced to a new language by writing the "Hello World" program. Hello World is traditionally a simple exercise that involves displaying the titular text on the screen. To do it in Python, we must open up our IDE or text editor and simply type the function.

print ("Hello, World!")

Next, we save the file. In IDLE (and most IDEs such as Atom) one must go through "file" and click "save as". In Nano ctrl+x must be pressed. Name the file with a ".py" extension and save it in an easily accessible directory- your desktop is perfectly fine. For this demonstration we will name the file "test.py".

Running a Python file differs slightly between platforms. Windows must use the command prompt, while Linux must use the terminal. Open up the respective application (ctrl+R and then cmd for Windows, ctrl+T for Linux). These applications are text-based interfaces that can be used to navigate and interact with a computer. The printed line will tell which directory you are currently located in, and you can type "dir" in Windows or "ls" in Linux to display a list of files in that directory. Move to another folder by typing "cd" followed by the directory name. Since we have saved the file to the desktop, on both operating systems we can make it active by typing "cd Desktop". Finally, the Hello World script can be run by typing "python test.py" or "python3 test.py" (on Linux).

If the above programming code was copied exactly, the output "Hello, World!" will be seen. The program will run and then exit back to terminal/prompt. Not entirely glamourous, but a worthy first step into learning Python.

Programming Concepts

In the above program, "print" is referred to as a command or function. Each function has a specific syntax that must be followed. For example, after print there is a set of parenthesis. Values passed within parenthesis are called parameters. Quotations also surround our text, and that is syntax that specifies written text, or a string. The syntax of print must be followed exactly, or else a syntax error will be returned when the program tries to run. As new functions are introduced in this book, careful attention must be placed upon following the syntax rules.

Anything can be put within the quotations of the print function and it will be written to the console. Since Python starts at the beginning of a script and reads lines individually, multiple print functions can be placed one after another like so:

print ("Hello, World!")

print ("This is my 2nd Python Program")

print ("Notice how each print command puts the text on a new line!")

After saving and running the file, all three functions will print their respective parameters. As mentioned previously, the quotations explain that text will be displayed. By forgoing quotations, numbers can be displayed instead.

print ("The answer to everything is:")

print (42)

    Python starts at the beginning of the script file and works its way down one line at a time until no more lines are found, in which case the program exits back to prompt or terminal.

Variables

Computers have the ability to "remember" data by storing the values as variables. Variables are RAM locations that are set aside to contain a value. Programming languages must specifically declare variables and assign them by writing code. Being able to manipulate data will prove to be a valuable asset when creating applications.

Creating a variable is known as "declaration". Giving a value is known as "assigning". Python simplifies the process by combining the two concepts into a single statement. Within a program the following line will create a variable:

```
lucky_number = 7
```

And then we can use the print function to view the variable we created.

print (lucky_number)

Because Python starts at the top of a program and works downwards, the above lines need to be in the correct order. If lucky_number is not first created, then print() will return an error for attempting to call a variable that does not yet exist.

An important distinction that can be made is seen when closely viewing the previous print() parameter. The variable lucky_number is not placed within quotations, so Python knows to print the value contained within (7). If we placed quotations around the text, Python would print "lucky_number", which was not our intended result. This situation is referred to as a logic error.

Variable Types

Variables can contain values of multiple types. Our first variable was assigned a numerical value, but Python has methods for handling values of different types as well.

secret_message = "rosebud"

print (secret_message)

As shown above, we can assign a string of text to a variable as well. The process is nearly the same, but notice the quotations around the value that explicitly indicate a string. Here are the most important data types in Python 3:

- Integer – Simple numerical value as a whole number.
    - 1, 0, -7

- Float – Decimal value. "Floating Point Number".
    - 3.0, -7.6, 1.0100001

- String – Letters, words, or entire phrases. Contained within quotation marks.
    - "Hello, world", "no", "12"

- Lists/Tuples/Dictionaries – Multiple related values grouped together as one object. Can be a variety of data types.
    - [1, 4, 4, 0], ["Dog", 2, "yes"]

Obviously, numerical values are declared by simply supplying an integer in the variable declaration. If there is a decimal involved, it will a float. Quotations signify strings, and brackets are for lists.

Variables can also be used in equations, or altered and changed mid-program. Write the following lines to a script.

first_num = 2

result = 3 + first_num

print (result)

first_num = 3

result = 3 + first_num

print (result)

You can observe that the value 2 is assigned to first_num. Then, we create a new variable "result" that is equal to a short mathematical expression. 3 and 2 are added and assigned to the result, which is printed as 5. Then, first_num is updated to contain a new value. Result is calculated again and the new result is printed out. This program shows how easy it is to use variables within assignments, and how variables can be edited at any time in the program.

More arithmetic operations can be done to numerical variables by specifying an operator in the equation. The following list explains the 5 main operators and the symbol that is used to perform the sequence.

- Addition (+) – Combining numbers

- Subtraction (-) – Taking the difference of numbers

- Multiplication (*) – Repeated addition

- Division (/) – Grouping, or the opposite of multiplication

- Modulus (%) – Dividing and using the remainder as an answer

Both integers and floats can easily perform calculations using the above operators. Note, though, that integers will generally return integer answers (whole numbers) while floats will always return an answer with a decimal point. Python can usually transform an integer into a float when it is needed, but good programming form comes from choosing the correct data type at the appropriate time. For example, see how floats are used in the program below:

first_number = 5.0

second_number = 3.0

```
result = first_number / second_number
```

```
print (result)
```

And the console will return 1.666666 as an answer. Whereas if integers were used everything past the decimal would be left off for an answer of 1. Assigning the answer to the result variable is not entirely necessary in our small program, and we can rewrite it like so:

```
first_number = 5.0
```

```
second_number = 3.0
```

print (first_number / second_number)

      String variables are not edited mathematically (as in 1 + "two" would not return 3). Instead, the remarks are changed by simply overwriting the words.

name = "Bob"

name = "Bill"

print (name)

Name will initially be created as the string "Bob", but "Bill" is assigned to it directly after. So when print() is called, the string only contains "Bill". Operators can be used, however, to combine separate strings.

my_string = "Hello,"

my_string2 = "World! "

print (my_string + my_string2)

print (my_string2 * 3)

The output would be "Hello, World!" for the first print(), and "World!

World! World!" for the second print(). The addition operator combines two strings together into one massive string, and the multiplication operator repeats a string the specified number of times.

Input

Although what we have learned so far is interesting, predetermined applications are not very useful for the end user. Python allows us, though, to obtain input from the user to add a layer of interactivity within our scripts. The input() function assigns input to a variable.

favorite_number = input ("What is your favorite number? ")

When a program reaches this line, it will display the text specified and wait for user input. Whatever is input will be assigned to favorite_number, which can be called just as any other variable.

print ("Your favorite number is", favorite_number)

Instead of using an addition operand, we use a comma instead. In print(), commas are used to combine multiple print statements into one (on the same line). We could have used either method, but operators cannot be used for differing data types. Both data types are strings in this case, so it all still works.

The answer that the user gives through input() will always be a string, though. If we were seeking a numerical answer we would have to convert it. Another function, int() can be used to extract numerical data from a string.

favorite_number = int(input ("What is your favorite number? "))

print ("Your favorite number plus 2 is ", favorite_number + 2)

There are a lot of new nuances going on in this program. For example, int() is used to convert the input into an integer. Notice how int() surrounds the entire input() function, which happens because input() must be passed as the entire parameter of int(). Next, the print statement is printing multiple bits of output, and the equation "favorite_number + 2" is evaluated before being printed.

Using int() will always return an integer answer, but float() could have been used to extract a decimal answer instead. The int() function works essentially by transforming the string "3" into the number 3. Definitely remember to include it whenever getting numerical input.

String Formatting

Being able to display strings with print() is useful, but sometimes our programs require us to display variables within them. To actually insert a variable into a string without first editing it or combining multiple variables, we can use a "string formatter". The format() function can be included within a print() statement to do positional formatting of variables.

dog_name = "Rex"

print ("My dog's name is {} and he is a good boy.".format(dog_name))

When you run the above code, it automatically replaced the brackets {} with the supplied variable. The format() is placed directly after the string it will be editing, and before the closing parenthesis. So when the code is run, the console outputs "My dog's name is Rex...". Without using format(), we would have had to use a multi-line complicated print setup. But format()'s greatest use comes from situations with multiple variables.

dog_name = "Rex"

dog_age = 12

print ("My dog's name is {0} and he is {1}. Sit, {0}!".format(dog_name, dog_age))

Here we choose to specify values within the curly brackets. 0 translates to the first supplied parameter, while 1 refers to the second variable. Therefore anywhere in our string we can use {0} to have dog_name be inserted and {1} to have dog_age be inserted. The console text will be "My dog's name is Rex and he is 12. Sit, Rex!"

Example Program 1 – project1.py

```python
user_name = input("What is your name? ")



user_age = int(input("What is your age? "))



user_pets = int(input("How many pets do you have? "))



user_GPA = float(input("what is your GPA? "))



print () #print a blank line
```

print ("{0} is {1} years old. They have a {3} GPA, probably because they have {2} pets.".format(user_name, user_age, user_pets, user_GPA))

This program combines what we have learned so far to obtain input from the user and display it back to them. A new concept, comments are introduced as well. The # symbol is used to denote a comment, or a block of text for human reading. Whenever a # is placed on a line everything after it is ignored by Python. Comments are used primarily to explain things to other programmers that might happen to read your code. In our case, we explain that a blank print() line simply produces a blank line. It is good programming form to use comments throughout your code to explain potentially confusing elements or help remind yourself of what certain blocks of code are doing.

Next, the format() function is used to replace 4 different instances within a print() function. As you might have noticed, counting begins with 0 in Python. 0 always refers to the first element of something, which is why 3 indicates the fourth supplied variable in our format().

Depending upon the medium in which you are reading this publication, some of the above lines may have word-wrapped to multiple lines. This is not how you should be typing it into a text editor though, as the print() line is one single command. Furthermore, copy and pasting from this document may introduce extra characters that Python does not understand. Therefore the correct way to input project 1's code is by typing it out yourself.

Homework program:

- Make a program that obtains information about a user's pet and returns it back.

Decision Structures

Now that the basics of Python 3 are explained, we can begin to offer truly interactive programs by implementing decision structures into our code. Decision structures are pieces of code (called conditional statements) that evaluate an expression and branch the program down differing paths based on the outcome. Observe the following example:

```
user_input = int(input("What is 4 / 2? "))


if (user_input == 2):

    print ("Correct!")
```

else:

    print ("Incorrect...")

    First we obtain input from the user. We test user_input against 2 (the correct answer). If the conditional statement turns out true, then the program will print "Correct!". However, if the user provides the wrong answer Python will return "Incorrect...". There is a lot of new concepts going on here, so we will break it down line by line.

    The first line is familiar to us; it obtains input, converting it into an integer and assigning it to the variable user_input. Line 2 introduces a new function- an "if statement". If statements are conditionals that evaluate the expression contained within the parenthesis. Our exact statement checks to see if user_input is 2, and if it is than the immediately following line of code is run. Comparisons use the "==" operator instead of the "=" operator. Double equal signs are checking for equality while single equal signs are only used to assign variables. Lastly, a colon follows the if statement.

    Indentations are used extensively in Python to separate off blocks of code. Under the if statement is a tabbed line with a print() function. Because this line is tabbed in, it will not run normally in code. Rather, the line will only run if the conditional if statement is proven true. Because our user input 3 the conditional will evaluate to "False" and the "Correct!" line will not run. Instead the program moves on to the "else statement". Else is a keyword that means "run when the if statement fails". Another indented line follows the conditional, but this time the indented code actually runs because else becomes activated.

If the user had input the correct answer of 2 instead, the if statement would evaluate to true and the console would print "Correct". In that situation, the else statement would not run at all. Focus once again on the indented code and understand that those lines are indented because they are part of the "if" and "else" code blocks. Also realize that only one statement from a decision structure can ever run in a program, so if "else" runs, that means "if" did not run. Likewise a program that has "if" activated will not run the code block under "else". Conditional statements are not limited to single lines of code, as you can see below.

```
user_input = input("What language is this written in? ")
```

```
if (user_input == "Python"):

    print ("Correct!")

else:

    print ("Incorrect...")

    print ("This is not written in {}, it uses Python!".format(user_input))
```

Another indented line is within the else code block, and both lines will run if the user does not correctly input "Python". This program does indeed compare strings, so quotations must surround the text.

Conditional Operators

Double equal signs (==) are only one of the many operators that can be used to create a conditional expression. This small list shows other operators in Python.

- \> - Greater than

- < - Less than

- == - Equal to

- >= - Greater than or equal to

- <= - Less than or equal to

- != - Not equal to

If statements evaluate whether the expression in the parenthesis is true; the above operators allow for some interesting expressions.

age = int(input("How old are you? "))

if (age <= 18):

    print ("Starting early! Good for you!")
else:

print ("Ah, a good age to learn.")

print ("Thank you for downloading this book.")

    A clever use of indentations is used here. If the user's age is 18 or under, it will congratulate them then skip the else statement and finally print out the thank you message. If the user is above 18 it will display the else message and then also thank them. No matter which conditional runs, the user will still receive the thank you message. The indentation makes all the difference about what code lines will actually run within a decision structure, and you must pay close attention to avoid a logic error.

For situations that require more than just two potential outcomes, the keyword "elif" can be used.

```
age = int(input("How old are you? "))

if (age <= 18 and age > 0):

    print ("Starting early!  Good for you!")

elif (age >= 80):

    print ("Never too late to learn!")
```

```
elif (age > 18 and age < 80):

    print ("Ah, a good age to learn.")

else:

    print ("That seems like an invalid age.")
    quit()


print ("Thank you for downloading this book.")
```

Elif is a keyword that can be used to split the decision making process into multiple branching paths. Between if and else statements, any number of elif conditionals can be used. Also, another new keyword is used above- "and". Our first comparison checks to see if age is less than or equal to 18 AND greater than 0. Therefore that conditional will only evaluate to true if the age value satisfies both requirements. Pretend the user input 75. The first statement evaluates, and 75 is indeed greater than 0, but it is not also less than 18, so that statement is skipped. Then, the first elif is evaluated. Age is not greater than 80, so that statement is skipped as well. Thirdly, age is definitely between 18 and 80, so the console prints "Ah, a good age to learn" and then skips the else statement altogether.

Remembering that only one statement in a decision "tree" can ever run, we can see that any elif that activates essentially runs its code block and then breaks from the decision structure. Else is used as a "catch-all" type expression in our above program. Any invalid input, such as "-1" would be picked up by else and displayed as such. Good programming form comes from catching potential user errors like this, and as an aspiring programmer you should always be expecting the user to incorrectly input values whenever the chance arises.

"And" is a comparison operator that forces both parts of an expression to be true. Another operator, "or", is used to force only one part of the expression to evaluate to true.

elif (age == 25 or age == 50 or age == 75):

print ("Happy quarterly birthday!")

If we were to put this elif within the above program (under the first if), we would see that only one part of the expression must be true for the whole comparison to be true. The user's age could be 25, 50, or 75 and the application would say "Happy quarterly birthday". Using "and" instead of "or" would be impossible, because the age cannot be 25 and 50 and 75 all at the same time. The keywords that we use for comparisons are helpful and greatly useful, but if used incorrectly they can lead to logic errors.

Example Program 2 – project2.py

```python
print("Python Quiz!")

answered = 0

correct = 0

print()

print("What version of python are we using?")
```

```python
print("A: 1, B: 2, C: 3")

user_answer = input("Enter A, B, or C: ")

answered += 1

print()

if (user_answer == "C" or user_answer == "c"):
    correct += 1
```

```
    print ("Correct")

else:

    print ("Incorrect")

print()


print("How many 'else' statements can be in a decision tree?")


print("A: 1, B: Infiniate, C: None")
```

```
user_answer = input("Enter A, B, or C: ")



answered += 1



print()



if (user_answer == "A" or user_answer == "a"):


    correct += 1


    print ("Correct")
```

```
else:

    print ("Incorrect")


print()


print("What does '=' do in Python?")


print("A: Compare, B: Assign, C: Both")


user_answer = input("Enter A, B, or C: ")


answered += 1
```

```
print()



if (user_answer == "B" or user_answer == "b"):



    correct += 1



    print ("Correct")



else:



    print ("Incorrect")
```

```
print()



print ("You got {} out of {} correct.".format(correct, answered))



if (correct == 3):


    print ("Congratulations!  Good score.")



elif (correct == 2):


    print ("Good work, but study hard!")
```

else:

   print ("Go back and read over the section again, I'm sure you'll get it.")

Homework program:

- Use if statements to create a calculator program that prompts the user for two numbers and an operator.

Loops

Just as conditional statements activate if an expression evaluates to true, looping conditionals also compare values in an expression. But while if, elif, and else statements are linear in nature, other conditionals have the ability to repeatedly run blocks of code. "Loops" are conditional statements that can be run several times through the course of a program, and they allow for expanded functionality within Python programs. A "while" loop is such a conditional.

```
answer = 0
```

```
while (answer != 2):
```

```
answer = int(input("What is 4 / 2? "))
```

```
print ("Correct!")
```

So long as the specified condition evaluates to true, the "while" code block will continuously run. We can see a perfect example of this through the program above. We create a new variable "answer" and repeatedly compare it to 2. While answer is not equal to 2, the program will ask the user for the correct answer. Inputting something other than 2 will just loop back around to the while statement, again prompting for the correct answer. If while finally does evaluate to true (because answer equals 2) the loop will break and the program will resume by printing "Correct".

The program can be enhanced further by "nesting" conditionals. A single indentation indicates a code block set aside for our while statement, but we can go for a second level of indentation to add an additional comparison.

```
answer = 0

while (answer != 2):

    answer = int(input("What is 4 / 2? "))

    if (answer != 2):

        print ("Incorrect...")
```

print ("Correct!")

      This program uses "nested" functions to incorporate if statements within while statements. The sheer amount of possibilities gained from this are virtually endless. Note how there are indentation levels that determine which code blocks can run within which functions. Every intended block, both 1 and 2 indent levels, will run when the while loop activates. It is a hard-to-master concept, but one that surely increases functionality.

      Another common loop is the "for" loop. For is different from while in that a for loop runs through a range of numbers or a set of values instead of checking a conditional.

for user_variable in range (1, 5):

print (user_variable)

For takes the specified variable "user_variable" and uses the supplied range. The variable will be initialized at 1, and it will be iterated every time the function loops. By observing the output we can see how this works.

1

2

3

4

User_variable is printed out, then incremented to 2. It is printed again and incremented as 3. Once more time for 4. But it reaches 5 and stops, which is why 5 does not get printed out. Because the keyword "range" was used, the for loop will always start at the first number and stop at the second. Leaving it out will have the for loop cycle through the values given.

for user_variable in (1, 5):

print (user_variable)

For example, only "range" is left out here, but the output is very different.

1

5

Python runs the loop with the first value, 1, and then runs it with the second value, 5. We will learn that using for loops this way is especially useful for lists, dictionaries, and tuples.

Lastly, loops can be broken with the break() function. Bad programming form can lead to infinite loops, but including break() as a safeguard might save a user's computer from crashing.

Example Program 3 – project3.py

```python
print("Adding simulator")

print("Type a number to add to total, or type blank line to stop")

line = "a"

total = 0

while (line != ""):
```

```
line = input("")
```

```
if (line == ""):
```

```
    break
```

```
total += int(line)
```

```
print ("Total = {}".format(total))
```

Homework program:

- Write a program using if statements that displays a text adventure game. Offer multiple choices to the player that they can type in to select. Use while loops to check the validity of user input.

More about Variables

Lists are another data type beneficial to talk about. A list is an array of values that are grouped together into a single variable. The single variable can then be used to call upon any of the "sub variables" it contains. They are mostly used for organization and grouping purposes, and also to keep related variables in a similar place. List variables are created by initializing them.

state = "Texas"

jack_info = [8, "West Elementary", state, "A"]

```
print ("Jack goes to {} in
{}.".format(jack_info[1], jack_info[2]))
```

```
print ("He has a {} in math, even though
he's only {}.".format(jack_info[3],
jack_info[0]))
```

The list "jack_info" contains four values because we specify four different entries between the square brackets. They are just ordinary values such as the integer 8 or the variable state, but they are grouped together for a common purpose by being placed into the list. As it is seen, entries in lists can be accessed by specifying the location of the entry in square brackets. Counting starts at 0, so the first entry of jack_info is 8, and the entry in [3] is "A". Visualize it like so:

Entry number:	0	1	2	3

| Data value: | 8 | "West Elementary" | state | "A" |

A list could be initially declared with 3 entries, and it would have the range 0-2. The number of entries is nearly infinite, and it is only limited by the computer's memory and the amount of variables the programmer fills it with.

The elements of a list can be edited as if they were individual variables. If Jack ages a year, we only need to update the entry. Furthermore, adding a new entry to the list can be done without completely redefining every value within it. Using append(), a new entry will be created in the last

state = "Texas"

```python
jack_info = [8, "West Elementary", state, "A"]



jack_info[0] = 9



jack_info.append(22)



print ("Jack goes to {} in {}.".format(jack_info[1], jack_info[2]))


print ("He has a {} in math, even though he's only {}.".format(jack_info[3], jack_info[0]))
```

```
print ("Lucky number is
{}".format(jack_info[4]))
```

The new additions to the program change the list ever so slightly to now have a new set of values.

Entry number:	0	1	2	3	4
Data value:	9	"West Elementary"	state	"A"	22

Before continuing onwards, it is worthy to note a few more features about the string data type. Strings are actually lists that contain character values. As an example, take the string "Hello, World!". Broken down as a list, it would look like this:

Entry	0	1	2	3	4	5	6	7	...
Character	H	e	l	l	o	,		W	...

And likewise, individual entries can be displayed from the string list.

print (user_string[0]) # would print "H"

print (user_string[7:13]) #would print "World!"

Moving onwards, tuples are another data type within Python. They are declared by using parentheses instead of square brackets. Tuples are actually static lists, or lists that cannot be edited. They are used when the programmer needs to ensure a range of data cannot change.

jim_grades = (99, 87, 100, 99, 77)

print (jim_grades[2])

Notice how an entry in a tuple is still accessed using square brackets.

Dictionaries take the concept of organized variables and take it to an extreme. Just like lists and tuples, dictionaries can contain multiple values in a single variable. The difference, however, is that dictionaries organize their records through names instead of numbers. In this way, dictionaries are "unordered" lists of sorts, where any value can be called by the entry name.

Declare a dictionary with curly brackets, separating out values with commas and colons.

pet_dict = {"Total": 2, "Dog": "Scruffy", "Cat": "Meowzer"}

print ("I have {} pets, {} and {}".format(pet_dict["Total"], pet_dict["Dog"], pet_dict["Cat"]))

  Here, the dictionary pet_dict contains three values: "Total", "Dog", and "Cat". The entries are declared by naming the entry within quotations and then supplying a value. Those entries are called by specifying the name of the entry, such as with pet_dict["Dog"] to access the value stored within. An unprecedented amount of organization is available when using dictionaries because they resemble a database in form. Likewise, they can be changed, updated, removed, or added to at any time within a program.

```
albums = {"Milkduds": 2, "Harold Gene": 1, "The 7750's": 3}
```

```
albums["Milkduds"] += 1 #new album!
```

```
albums["The 7750's"] = 2 #actually only had 2
```

```
albums.update({"Diamond Dozens": 1}) #found new band
```

```
del albums["Harold Gene"] #sold one away, didn't like
```

print ("These are the number of albums I own:")

print (albums)

The humorous example above is a simple dictionary used to store the number of albums a person has. At the beginning the dictionary has a set number of albums for each band, but the second line has the collector gaining a new Milkduds album. That line also uses a new code shortcut. Whenever "+=" is used, the code is actually expanded to be "albums["Milkduds"] = albums["Milkduds"] + 1", but much time and space is saved in the program by using the shorthand. Third line has the collector realizing they only had 2 7750's albums, so the command changes the value of the entry altogether. Next update() is introduced. It shows how an entirely new entry can be added to the dictionary. Sadly, though, Harold Gene is deleted from the dictionary because the collector sold away the album. Finally, printing the entire dictionary can be done by not specifying any entry.

     A fun example, the above program actually shows how versatile dictionaries can be in gathering and storing data. Include them within your program to group variables together in an easy-to-call way.

Example Program 4 – project4.py

```python
keep_going = "a" #initialize variables before they are used

number_grades = 0

grade_list = []

total = 0

print("Grade Average Calculator")
```

```
print()



while (keep_going != "No" and
keep_going != "no"):



    grade = int(input("Enter a test grade: "))



    number_grades += 1



    grade_list.append(grade)



    keep_going = input("Add more grades? ")
```

```
print()


for x in range (0, number_grades):


    total += grade_list[x] #add up all grades in list


print ("Average of {} tests is {}".format(number_grades, total / number_grades))
```

Homework program:

- Devise code for more math functions, such as medians and modes.

Functions

Every function used thus far has been built-in to Python and programmed by Python's developers. Functions are actually code shortcuts, as functions are condensed versions of code that take data as parameters, run longer blocks of code behind the scenes, and then return a result. The use of functions is to save time and code when doing commonly repeated tasks. Python retains the ability for programmers to write their own functions, and they are done like so:

def happy(name):

print ("Happy birthday to you. " * 2)

```
print ("Happy birthday dear {}.".format(name))
```

```
print ("Happy birthday to you.")
```

The "def" keyword indicates a user defined function declaration, and the name immediately following is the name of the function; we create the function happy(). Within the parentheses are the values that our function will take (only one, a variable named "name"). Just as print() must have a value, so does our happy() need one too. Then, the code associated with the function is indented. Our code simply runs through a happy birthday song, which supplying the variable "name" inside the song. This function declaration goes at the top of our python program, but it does not actually run when the program starts. To call it, we need to specifically reference the function in code.

happy("Dana")

Something interesting happens here. We call happy() by passing "Dana" as the value. "Dana" gets assigned to "name", and the function runs through. However, the variable "name" does not exist outside of the user defined function, and any attempts to call it will result in an error. This is because variables have scopes of operation, which are areas in which they can be accessed. "Name" has a variable scope that is specific to the function, so it will not ever be called outside of it. Similarly, any variables declared in the main program cannot directly be accessed by the user defined function, but rather they must be passed as parameters when calling the function. Follow along with the next exercise to see an example for an in-depth analysis on user defined functions (UDFs).

```python
def intdiv(num_one, num_two):

    whole_answer = int(num_one / num_two)


    remainder = num_one % num_two


    print ("{} / {} = {} with {} left over.".format(num_one, num_two, whole_answer, remainder))


first = int(input("Enter first number: "))
```

second = int(input("Enter second number: "))

intdiv(first, second)

  First, the UDF is declared. This code does not run automatically because it has not yet been called. The program actually starts on the fifth line. The variable "first" is declared within the main program's scope based on the user's input. So too is the variable "second". The UDF "intdiv" is invoked with first and second as the two parameters. The variables are passed as parameters so they can be transferred into the UDF. First and second are not actually leaving their scope, though, because the UDF uses the variables num_one and num_two to perform calculations.

Variables can be passed back from a UDF by using the return keyword.

```
def exp (base, pow):

    orig_num = base

    for x in range (1, pow):

        base = base * orig_num

    return base
```

Above is a UDF that calculates the result of exponential multiplication based on two supplied values, the base and power numbers. The return keyword passes a variable back into the main program, which is how we can get around the variable's scope.

answer = exp(2, 3)

So when we call the function like above, the answer (base) is given back as the result and assigned to the variable "answer".

Conclusively, user defined functions can save a lot of time for programs that must repeatedly call a block of code. UDFs can just contain other functions, like our Happy Birthday UDF, or they can help simplify complicated code, such as our exponential multiplication UDF. You must remember that variables are defined within a scope that they cannot leave. However, values can be passed from the main program to a UDF by supplying them as parameters, and values can return from a UDF by using the return keyword and assigning the result to a variable.

Example Program 5 – project5.py

```python
def cm_to_inch(cm):

    inch = cm * 0.39

    return inch


def inch_to_cm(inch):

    cm = inch * 2.54
```

```
    return cm


print("Inch/cm converter")


print("1: Convert cm to inch")


print("2: Convert inch to cm")


choice = int(input("Enter a menu option: "))


while (choice != 1 and choice != 2):

    print("Invalid, try again.")
```

```python
choice = int(input("Enter a menu option: "))



if (choice == 1):



    user_input = int(input("Enter cm: "))



    print("{} cm is {} inches.".format(user_input, cm_to_inch(user_input)))



if (choice == 2):
```

```python
    user_input = int(input("Enter inches: "))

    print("{} inches is {} cm.".format(user_input, inch_to_cm(user_input)))
```

print("Thank you for using the program.")

Homework program:

- Convert the programs you have already made to use UDFs

Classes

Classes are a feature of Python that bring it more in line with some of the more difficult programming languages. They are essentially "programs within programs" because of how many features you can put into one. Moreover, it is good programming form to use classes for organization. Object-oriented languages such as Python occasionally show their object roots through concepts like these, whereas objects contain attributes in the form "object.attribute". See the example below to understand.

class student:

    def __init__(self, name, grade):

self.name = name

self.grade = grade

self.gpa = 0.0

The class that we create is called "student", and student contains its own variables. Classes give us a way to organize objects and give them personal attributes. So instead of having student1_name, student1_grade, student2_grade, etc… as different variables, they can be consolidated by belonging to a class. Within a program, the class declaration goes at the very top. Just like a UDF, it does not actually run in the main program until called.

student1 = student("Tim", "Freshman")
#object is student1, an attribute is "name".

Our newly declared "student" class is used to create the student1 object with the attributes "Tim" and "Freshman". This would have previously taken two lines, but it is condensed considerably with classes. Classes compartmentalize the related variables of the object so that each "student" declared has the 3 properties "name", "grade", and "gpa". The second line of our class declaration contains __init__, which is a "method" (user defined function) that runs when an object in the student class is created. Init's parameters are the ones required when creating that object. Self is not actually a parameter, it just refers to "student", but "name" and "grade" are required, which is why we included them when creating "student1". Attributes of student1 can be called like so:

print (student1.name)

Which would simply print "Tim". We did not declare the GPA variable during the student1 initialization, so we can do that with an assignment statement.

student1.gpa = 4.0

Or otherwise change an attribute that already exists.

student1.grade = "Sophomore"

If we were to create another object, it would have its own set of attributes that are completely different from student1.

student2 = student("Mary", "Senior")

Where student1.grade is different from student2.grade, even though they share the same variable name. For large projects with multiple repeating variables, classes can reduce the amount of code clutter and variable names to keep track of.

Looking back to our custom class, we can expand upon it to achieve user defined functions within the class itself.

class student:

    def __init__(self, name, grade):

```
        self.name = name



        self.grade = grade



        self.gpa = 0.0



    def record(self):



        return "Student {} is a {} with a {}".format(self.name, self.grade, self.gpa)



student3 = student("Lily", "Junior")
```

student3.gpa = 3.67

print (student3.record())

The __init__ stays the same, but we add a UDF definition with the name "record". It passes the parameter self (because it has to refer to the class) and returns a formatted string. In our actual main program student3 is created. Finally, we call the UDF with student3.record() (object.function). It returns our formatted string, and therefore it is printed out by print().

Special Methods

The __init__ method is actually a form of a UDF. However, methods that are surrounded by two underscores are special methods within Python, which means they run automatically at certain times. __init__ is a special method also specifically called a "constructor method". Constructor methods get called whenever an object is created, and that is why we put variable declarations within it. When student3 is created, so too are student3.name, student3.grade, and student3.gpa. Therefore, any code that is put within the __init__ block will be activated any time an object is created for the first time.

Other special methods exist, and they are called on different events.

- __del__ - called whenever an object is deleted (del). Also called destructor method.

- __str__ - called when an object is passed as a string

- __setattr__ - will run every time an attribute is set with a value

- __delattr__ - same as setattr, but only runs when an attribute is deleted

Adding in these special methods can show when they run.

```python
class student:

    def __init__(self, name, grade):

        self.name = name
        self.grade = grade


        self.gpa = 0.0


    def __str__(self):


        return "{}".format(self.name)
```

def record(self):

    return "Student {} is a {} with a {}".format(self.name, self.grade, self.gpa)

student4 = student("Barry", "Professor")

print (student4)

When student4 is printed (referenced as a string), the __str__ special method takes over and returns the "name" attribute of the object. If this special method was not in there, we would not get the intended output from referencing the object.

Finally, classes are useful because we can create "class variables" within them. "Name" and "GPA" are attribute variables that are specific to each object declared, but there can also be class variables that are shared by all objects. For instance, this program will keep track of the total number of objects using a class variable.

```
class food:

    total_foods = 0

    def __init__(self, name):

        self.name = name
```

```
        self.calories = 0



        self.foodgroup = ""



        food.total_foods += 1



    def __del__(self):



        food.total_foods -= 1



    def __str__(self):
```

```
        return "{}".format(self.name)



    def get_total():



        return food.total_foods



    def record(self):



        return "Food {0} is a {2} with {1} calories.".format(self.name, self.calories, self.foodgroup)



food1 = food("Carrot Stew")
```

```
food1.calories = 210

food1.foodgroup = "Vegetables"

food2 = food("Buttered Toast")

food2.calories = 100

food2.foodgroup = "Grains"

print (food.get_total())
```

del food2

print (food.get_total())

As the program creates a food, 1 is added to total_foods. Then, a food object is deleted so 1 is taken away. The console prints 2, then 1 to show how our UDF can be called to check the class variable. Keeping track of the number of something is a common use for class variables, but they are highly useful for other situations as well.

Example Program 6 – project6.py

```python
class house:

    def __init__(self, name, bedrooms, bathrooms, cost):

        self.name = name

        self.bedrooms = bedrooms

        self.bathrooms = bathrooms
```

self.cost = cost

print("House for sale!")

def __del__(self):

print("House off the market.")

print("House for sale:")

user_input = input("What is the address of the house? ")

```python
user_input2 = int(input("How many bedrooms? "))




user_input3 = int(input("How many bathrooms? "))




user_input4 = int(input("How much does it cost? "))



house1 = house(user_input, user_input2, user_input3, user_input4)



print("Looking for buyers...")



for x in range (0, house1.cost):
```

x += 1 #wait a while

print("Sold!")

del house1

Homework program:

- Use classes to make a database organization program. Users should be able to create new entries of a class and set variables, and also view them at will.

Inheritance

In your more robust and expansive programs, you might use multiple related classes. As an example, think of the program where you must categorize devices on a network. Each device type (desktop, laptop, phone, etc...) will have its own class, but you will ultimately be repeating commonly used attributes. Both desktops and laptops will have names, departments, and IP addresses, but they will also have a few distinct variables specific to them such as Wi-Fi for the laptops and graphics cards for the desktop.

Through a process called "inheritance", classes can be put into a parent/child relationship where certain parent attributes can be "inherited" by children classes. Effectively sharing attributes across classes leads to more elegant organization and less code overall.

```python
class device:

    total_devices = 0

    def __init__(self, name, owner):

        self.name = name

        self.owner = owner

        device.total_devices += 1
```

```python
def __del__(self):

    device.total_devices -= 1

def __str__(self):

    return "{}".format(self.name)

def get_total():

    return device.total_devices
```

```python
class laptop(device):

    def __init__(self, name, owner, wifi):

        device.__init__(self, name, owner)
        self.wifi = wifi

    def __str__(self):

        return "{} is owned by {} and connected to {}".format(self.name, self.owner, self.wifi)


class cellular(device):
```

```python
def __init__(self, name, owner, connection, BYOD):

    device.__init__(self, name, owner)

    self.connection = connection

    self.BYOD = BYOD

def __str__(self):

    return "{} is owned by {} and it uses {}. BYOD? {}".format(self.name, self.owner, self.connection, self.BYOD)
```

```
device1 = laptop("STAFF12", "IT", "Staff-wifi")

device2 = cellular("Jack's-iDevice", "Jack", "4G LTE", "yes")

print (device1)

print (device2)

print (device.get_total())
```

In this program, the parent class "device" is created with 2 attributes – name and owner. The other classes, laptop and cellular, also contain name and owner attributes, so we set them up to inherit them from the parent class. To set a class into a parent/child relationship, the child class must pass the parent class as a parameter in the declaration. This is why "class cellular(device)" is used, because we are setting cellular to be linked to device.

Secondly, we call the device constructor method specifically within each child class constructor method. When this is done, the child class actually runs the entire parent constructor method. Name and owner are obtained this way, and also the "total_devices += 1" line gets passed as well.

Both children contain a __str__ method, even though the parent class also has one. Through a process called overwriting, if a special method is called that exists in both the parent and child, than only the child method will run. In the absence of a called method in a child, the parent will runs its method instead. This is why referencing a laptop object as a string will display laptop information, but deleting a laptop object will fall back to the parent and run its destructor method instead.

Understanding how inheritance works can provide your applications with unprecedented organization and composition. Most higher-level and advanced programs take advantage of classes and their properties to quickly devise a framework for many applications such as database tools, so learning them would undoubtedly improve your Python skills.

Example Program 7 – project7.py

```python
class house:

    def __init__(self, name, bedrooms, bathrooms):

        self.name = name

        self.bedrooms = bedrooms

        self.bathrooms = bathrooms
```

```
        self.cost = 0



        print("Living space for sale!")



    def __del__(self):



        print("Living space off the market.")



class apartment(house):



    def __init__(self, name, bedrooms, bathrooms):
```

house.__init__(self, name, bedrooms, bathrooms)

self.montly_payment = 0

forsale1 = apartment("100 Col. Ave", 2, 2)

forsale1.montly_payment = 250

Homework program:

- Expand the database program that you could optionally create in the last chapter to include inheritance.

Modules

Every bit of functionality that we have used so far is built-in to Python already. Python is an expansive language, but additional features can be added to Python easily through modules. Those familiar with C can relate modules to "h" files and preprocessor statements. Modules do much the same thing, they are included in order to add new functions and commands to Python.

To add a new module, we only need to include one statement at the top of our program.

import math

So in this line, we import the "math" module, which opens up a slew of new functions for us to use.

```
import math

print (math.sin(3))

answer = math.sqrt(16)

print (answer)

print (math.gcd(100, 125))
```

    In particular, sqrt(), sin(), and gcd() are three examples you can notice above. Every module has a defined purpose, and math's is to provide advanced mathematical functions. Here is a list of the most important ones.

- math.sqrt() – square root of number

- math.sin() – sine of number

- math.cos() – cosine of number

- math.tan() – tangent of number

- math.log() – two parameters, log and base

- math.pi – 3.14159

- math.e – 2.71828

Those needing to use complicated functions such as the ones above only need to "import math" at the top of the program.

Other specialized modules exist as well, such as datetime. Datetime is a module that provides time-keeping functions.

import datetime

current_time = datetime.datetime.now()

print (current_time.hour)

print (current_time.minute)

print (current_time.second)

Other functions provided through datetime include:

- year
- month
- day

Or os, a module that unlocks operating system functions for altering files. Here is a small program for creating a new folder and then making it the active directory.

import os

os.mkdir("folder") #make folder

os.chdir("folder") #go into folder

os.chdir("..") #up one directory

More functions available to os are listed.

- os.rmdir() – delete specified folder

- os.remove() – delete specified file

- os.path.exists() – checks to see if specified file exists

- os.rename() – renames specified file to second parameter supplied

And other highly useful modules, such as random, statistics, and pip exist that can give new features to your Python applications that were not previously possible. Python also has support for downloading and using user-created modules, but that is an advanced concept not covered here.

Example Program 8 – project8.py

```
import random

print ("Fortune telling...")

rng = random.randrange(1, 7)

if (rng == 1):

    print("You will soon come into money.")
```

```
elif (rng == 2):

    print("Consider buying stocks.")

elif (rng == 3):

    print("Look both ways before crossing.")

elif (rng == 4):

    print("Call your relatives...")
```

```
elif (rng == 5):

    print("You will get a phone call.")
else:

    print("Future cloudy... Try again.")
```

Homework project:

- Create a "sampler" program that shows off various Python module features.

Common Errors

Because many programmers choose Python as their first language to learn, they often succumb to a few common errors. If your applications are not functioning correctly, or if you are looking for a few of the best programming practices, than this section will help you. When code is run through Python, it may stop and return an error to you. By reading the error you can learn which line the error comes from, and usually Python will point (^) to the exact character that is wrong. Use the information that is given to you to understand your error and rectify the situation.

Not specifying the correct parameters is a common newbie mistake. When putting values between the parentheses for a function, you must pay close attention to what kind of data it expects. Some functions require only integers, and some have 2 or more parameters to enter. When in doubt, consult the Python documentation page for the specific function you are working with. Advanced IDEs, such as Atom and Eclipse often are programmed to display an example parameter list as you are typing out a function, and you can follow along with the example to know what each parameter is expecting.

Sometimes we forget to convert user input to an integer. If we are prompting a user for numerical input, we must surround input() with int() for float(). Failure to do this will pass the input as a string, which will likely return an error.

When comparing two values, Python requires the programmer to use the double equal sign (==). When assigning a value, you must use the single equal sign (=). Using an inappropriate sign for any occasion will always return a syntax error.

After every comparison statement and loop (such as if, elif, else, for, while, def, and class) there is a colon (:). This colon denotes that the next line should be indented, and thus all indented lines will fall within the function's scope. Failure to place a colon returns a syntax error.

Strings and functions are usually surrounded by a pair of characters. Functions use parentheses, while strings use quotations to indicate where their boundaries are. If you ever forget to supply the closing character, Python will surely return an error.

Beginners will often try to use functions that are not in Python by default without including the correct module. Trying to call an advanced math function, or editing a file directory is not possible with regular Python. Always place the import commands for modules you will use at the top of the program, or the application will simply not run.

Indentations are required in Python. Those coming from other programming languages will likely forget this and indent in their own personal style. This will break mostly all Python programs, because the interpreter expects a certain formatting standard. An error will be returned every time that indentations are incorrect. Pay close attention to your indentation levels or risk your program failing to logic and syntax errors.

Programming languages demand perfect syntax at all times. Because of this, even a spelling error can be disastrous for our applications. Besides indentation problems and misspelled functions, giving the wrong variable name or accidentally calling the wrong function can make your program fail outright or perform unexpectedly. When coding, double check over your scripts to ensure no characters are out of place. Test your code after each implementation so you know that when an error occurs it should be coming from a new addition. Sometimes there is an error or bug in the code and it just cannot be rectified after reviewing the code. Programmers must "debug" their code by following it line-by-line at this point, "tracing" the path that the interpreter takes as it runs the program. Some IDE's have tools for debugging, such as "breakpoints" or "line stops" that allow you to run each line at the click of a button. Taking the program slow like that can reveal the source of the issue most of the time, but it takes a keen eye and a dedicated troubleshooter to fix code.

    Many programmers consider it unnecessary, but commenting your scripts is an essential part of coding. Failure to do so is an extremely common beginner mistake that many first time programmers fall for. Once you master the art of Python and begin programming in a company with other coders, there might be multiple people working on the same script. Even the cleanest code is confusing to look at for the first time, but comments help to demystify the complex characters. Moreover, coming back to an old script of yours from weeks past can feel like reading a foreign language- comments help you to quickly get back to coding. Many programmers put a comment as the top line of their program with a brief description of what the script does, when it was written, and any contributors to it. That way the next time you are quickly looking through files trying to find a certain program, the comments can help you understand what is inside without actually running or deciphering the code.

    The final common mistake that runs rampant in Python newbies is variable naming. If it has not already been brought to light in your experimentation, there are just certain names that you cannot name your variables. "Reserved" words such as class, break, print, and, or, while, etc... are keywords that cannot be used for a variable name. If Python detects their use a syntax error will occur. Besides errors, though, programmers often use bad form when naming their variables. Avoid ambiguous and simple variable names such as "number" or "var1" in favor of descriptive one such as "user_input" or "totalNumberOfDogs". These variables explain their use at a glance, so a verbose programmer will never misuse a variable or have to check what its intent is. Python programmers typically use the underscore method to name their variables (grade_average, dog_1), but camelCase is acceptable as well (userInput, multAnswer). No matter which method is used, a skillful programmer will always make the name descriptive.

Conclusion

Thank you again for downloading this beginner's guide to Python. Now that you have finished the text, you have a basic knowledge of how Python works, and you should be able to write your own programs. You can further increase your knowledge by attempting to create larger and more complicated programs, or you can study modules and learn new functions. If you have enjoyed the book, rate and leave a review on Amazon so more high quality books can be produced.

Related Titles

[Hacking University: Freshman Edition Essential Beginner's Guide on How to Become an Amateur Hacker](#)

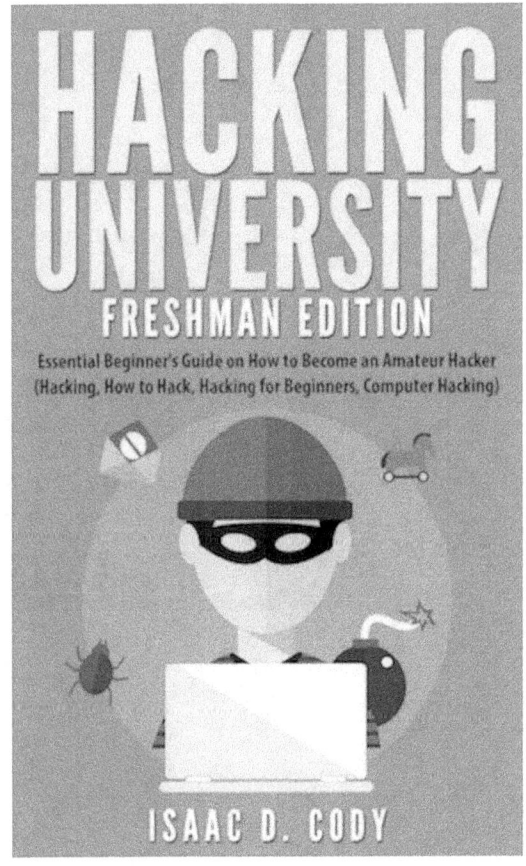

Hacking University: Sophomore Edition. Essential Guide to Take Your Hacking Skills to the Next Level. Hacking Mobile Devices, Tablets, Game Consoles, and Apps

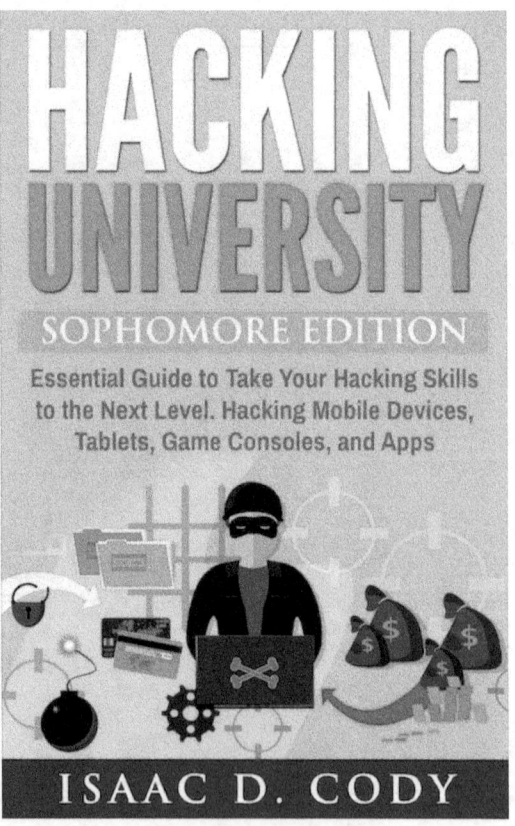

Hacking University: Junior Edition. Learn Python Computer Programming From Scratch. Become a Python Zero to Hero. The Ultimate Beginners Guide in Mastering the Python Language

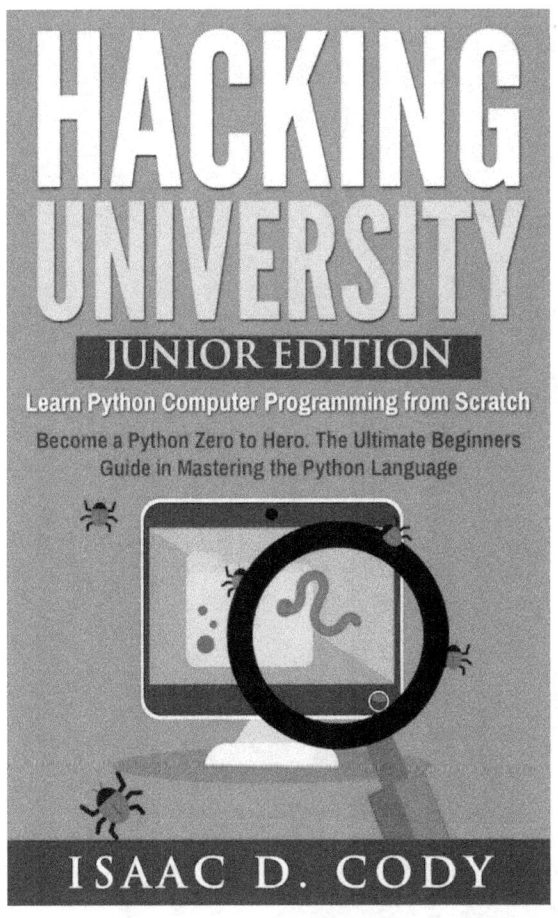

Hacking University: Senior Edition Linux. Optimal Beginner's Guide To Precisely Learn And Conquer The Linux Operating System. A Complete Step By Step Guide In How Linux Command Line Works

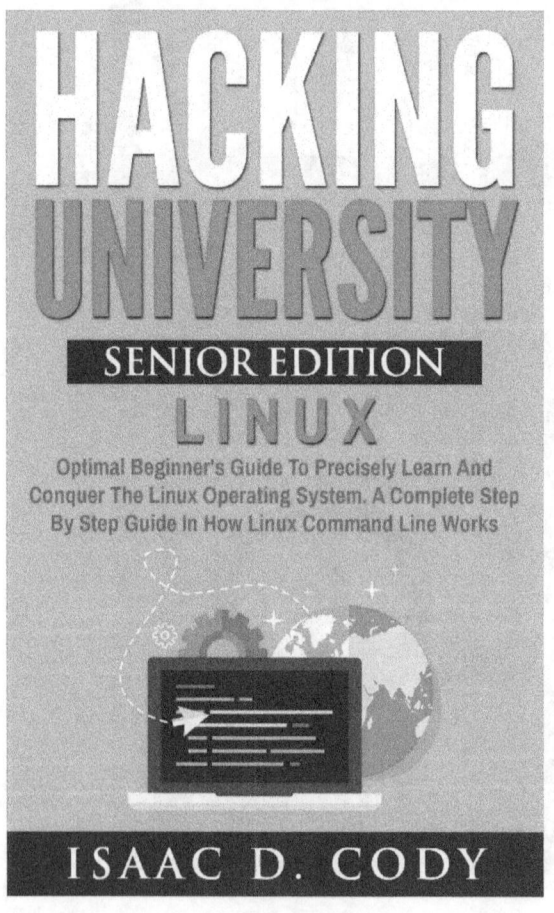

Hacking University: Graduation Edition.
4 Manuscripts (Computer, Mobile,
Python, & Linux). Hacking Computers,
Mobile Devices, Apps, Game Consoles
and Learn Python & Linux

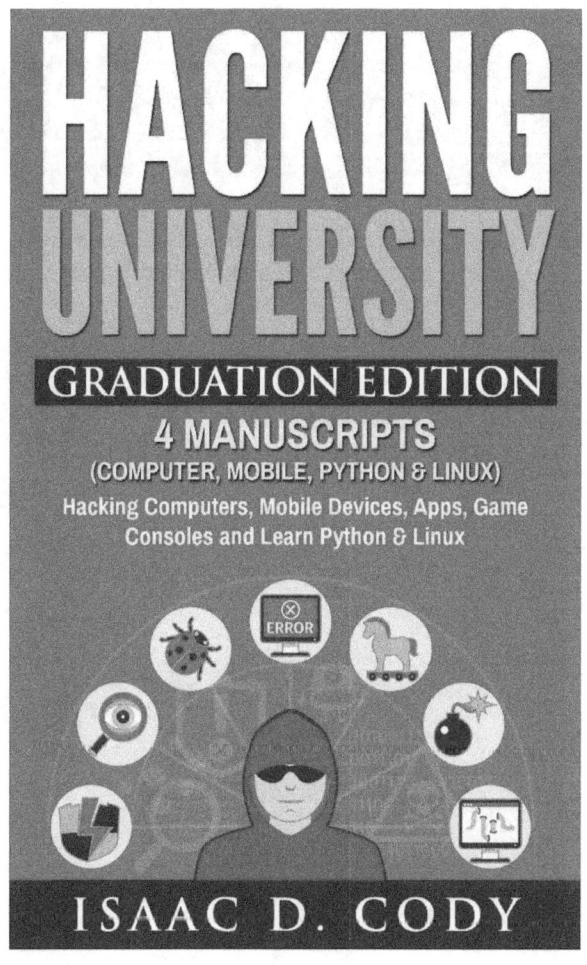

Data Analytics: Practical Data Analysis and Statistical Guide to Transform and Evolve Any Business, Leveraging the power of Data Analytics, Data Science, and Predictive Analytics for Beginners

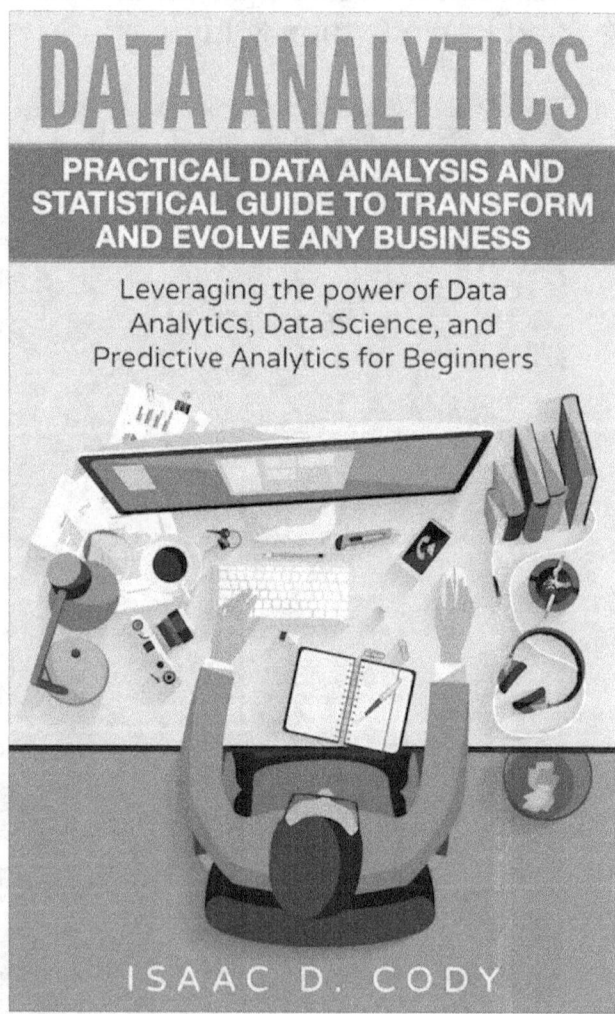

About the Author

Isaac D. Cody is a proud, savvy, and ethical hacker from New York City. After receiving a Bachelors of Science at Syracuse University, Isaac now works for a mid-size Informational Technology Firm in the heart of NYC. He aspires to work for the United States government as a security hacker, but also loves teaching others about the future of technology. Isaac firmly believes that the future will heavily rely computer "geeks" for both security and the successes of companies and future jobs alike. In his spare time, he loves to analyze and scrutinize everything about the game of basketball.

www.ingramcontent.com/pod-product-compliance
Lightning Source LLC
Chambersburg PA
CBHW071415180526
45170CB00001B/105